"This is an interesting examina
Svendsen's prose is familiar, easy to understand, and occasionally hilarious. Moving between solid scholarship and personal experience with ease, this book provides readers with a modern sense of both Loki and Sigyn."

—Patricia Lafayllve, author of
A Practical Heathen's Guide to Asatru

"*Loki and Sigyn* offers a comprehensive and sincere look at Loki, Sigyn, and their presence within inclusive Heathenry. With humor, affection, and insight, Lea Svendsen provides strong citations while staying personable, not pedantic, provides a platform for many perspectives while affirming care and devotion, and balances beginner-friendly overviews with fresh information even Lokean old-timers will find intriguing. Loki is my oathed beloved, and Svendsen's writing resonates with how I know and love him—and it's the attention offered to the goddess Sigyn, so frequently overlooked and misrepresented, that I appreciate most about this book. Svendsen's work is a much-needed contribution to this community."

—Bat Collazo, editor of *Blood Unbound: A Loki Devotional*

"Wait, was I not just sitting in a drinking hall listening to an excited Lokean drinking Jagermeister and telling stories while standing on a table? It certainly feels that way after reading *Loki and Sigyn*! I laughed, I cried, I found insightful commentary and a good mix of scholarship and gnosis. I also found the main stories—yes, they're very important (and funny)! But there were also lessons about bad decisions, accountability, love, devotion, and compassion as well. Oh, and let's not forget all the lessons on how to honor that fiery boi and his wife (there were plenty of those—don't forget the candy!). 10 out of 10 would recommend (and I don't even usually bother with the guy)."

—Cat Heath, author of *Elves, Witches, & Gods*

LOKI AND SIGYN

© Kathleen G. Kistler

ABOUT THE AUTHOR

Lea Svendsen has been accused of being "a mortician who's actually three foxes in a trench coat," "perpetually adjacent to catastrophe," "the Lokeanest Lokean who ever Lokeaned," and her grandfather's "little genius." She can't argue with any of them (except maybe Grandpa's contribution) as she embraces the chaotic life of dedication to Loki and Sigyn.

She's a generational heathen, but she's quick to point out that her practice is different from her father's, which in turn was different from his father's. In fact, her mother took it upon herself to shape Lea's Nordic philosophy and worldview and raise her with heathen values, despite not actually being heathen herself.

She is a proud member of the kindred Glitnir and humbled to be a part of the Northeast Heathen Community. When she's not looking for foxes and opossums in the woods or escaping to Iceland for coffee and rye bread ice cream at Cafe Loki, she's going down absurd rabbit holes online and researching morbid and obscure history and phenomenon.

Lea lives in eastern Pennsylvania with her beloved etymologist, two clingy cats, and a ghost. She hopes to add a ferret to the mix in honor of Loki.

You can read more about her Loki kinda life (and find out if she ever gets a ferret) at her site, LevLeLoki.com.

LOKI AND SIGYN

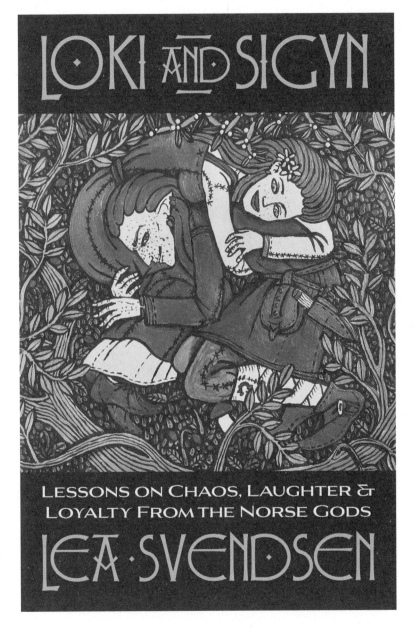

LESSONS ON CHAOS, LAUGHTER & LOYALTY FROM THE NORSE GODS

LEA SVENDSEN

LLEWELLYN PUBLICATIONS · WOODBURY, MINNESOTA

FIRST EDITION
Third Printing, 2024

Cover design by Kevin R. Brown
Cover illustration by Helena Rosová
Interior art by Llewellyn Art Department

Llewellyn Publications is a registered trademark of Llewellyn Worldwide Ltd.

Library of Congress Cataloging-in-Publication Data
Names: Svendsen, Lea, author.
Title: Loki and Sigyn : lessons on chaos, laughter & loyalty from the Norse gods / Lea Svendsen.
Description: First edition. | Woodbury, Minnesota : Llewellyn Publications, [2022] | Includes bibliographical references and index.
Identifiers: LCCN 2021051530 (print) | LCCN 2021051531 (ebook) | ISBN 9780738769318 (paperback) | ISBN 9780738769431 (ebook)
Subjects: LCSH: Loki (Norse deity) | Sigyn (Norse deity) | Mythology, Norse. | Neopaganism.
Classification: LCC BL870.L6 S84 2022 (print) | LCC BL870.L6 (ebook) | DDC 398.20936801—dc23/eng/20220103
LC record available at https://lccn.loc.gov/2021051530
LC ebook record available at https://lccn.loc.gov/2021051531

Llewellyn Worldwide Ltd. does not participate in, endorse, or have any authority or responsibility concerning private business transactions between our authors and the public.

All mail addressed to the author is forwarded but the publisher cannot, unless specifically instructed by the author, give out an address or phone number.

Any internet references contained in this work are current at publication time, but the publisher cannot guarantee that a specific location will continue to be maintained. Please refer to the publisher's website for links to authors' websites and other sources.

Llewellyn Publications
A Division of Llewellyn Worldwide Ltd.
2143 Wooddale Drive
Woodbury, MN 55125-2989
www.llewellyn.com

Printed in the United States of America

DEDICATION

For my champion and hero, Mom,
who raised me with all of the love and magic of folklore.

And for Steve, who exemplifies the best that Christianity has
to offer, but still loves his crazy heathen daughter anyway.

In Memoriam
Frank N. Svendsen
1919–2004
Thank you, Grandpa, for keeping the gods
close to us and us close to the gods.

— ◆ —

CONTENTS

ACKNOWLEDGEMENTS

Kevin, *ástin mín*: This book is your fault. If you hadn't launched into an impromptu lecture about the etymology of "Sigyn" and why it *isn't* Victory Woman, I wouldn't have reflected on why a devotional like this was needed. Your insights (and the help you gave translating obscure old Icelandic texts) have been invaluable and have deepened my own relationship with Loki and Sigyn. I'm glad this project deepened our relationship, too. Thanks again for wading through five-page-long footnotes for Loki's sake (and for mine).

Erika, who likes tacos: ECT '18 changed my life forever what with being hit with one impossible miracle after another. One of those miracles was you. "There she is," Loki whispered. "*She's the one you need to talk to.*" I felt horribly awkward approaching you to babble thanks for the work you did with Loki's vé, but if I hadn't been nudged to introduce myself, where would I be now? I'll tell you where: adrift and lost without my Star Dust Twin/ Soul Sibling/Sister Wife/Whatever We've Decided We Are. I just know my life is better with you in it. Thank you for contributing to this book for our boy. Go get you some tacos.

Mortellus: This book wouldn't be possible without you. I still cackle at the way we met mere hours after I declared my intention to write a devotional for Loki and Sigyn. It's like they said, "Finally! Let's make the magic happen!" And they did. They did this by bringing this Gardnerian Wiccan into my life, but Mortellus, you brought the magic. For that, I couldn't be more grateful! It's an honor to know you and call you my friend, Grammatically Precise Witch of the Morrigan.

Glitnir: I can't possibly tell you how much each of you mean to me. It's because of you that I met the rest of the NEHC, and it's because of you that I've been able to thrive. I'm humbled and thrilled to be counted among you, and *so proud* to call you my kin. In spirit of our motto, "Immolation is the sincerest form of flattery," I burn with love for each and every one of you!

Mom and Steve: I don't know how you put up with me and my constant nonsense. "Weird journey" doesn't come *close* to describing what I've put you two through. As many twists and turns as my life has taken, I'm thankful that you've both supported me every step of the way. Here's to the next adventure!

Northeast Heathen Community: I *still* can't believe I'm lucky enough to be counted among such an incredible community of amazing people. My life is exponentially better because of the knowledge, humor, and friendship we all share. I'm humbled by your support. Thank you for letting me be part of something so special. That goes double for my beloved Matt and Annie: I love you two always and forever.

And to my beloved Sigyn and Loki: Sigyn, despite your quiet nature you're certainly a powerhouse who isn't to be ignored. Thank you for teaching me how to bite, and to bite hard. And *you*. Truth-Forcer, World-Breaker. My world has certainly been broken, time and again. My body has been broken, and my heart has been broken. But thanks to you, my spirit has never broken. You have never left my side. While the course of my life has been chaotic and at times overwhelming, it's with the greatest pride and gratitude that I start this devotional with a gleeful HAIL LOKI!

FOREWORD

It was 2019 and I was in the throes of writing *"Do I Have To Wear Black? Rituals, Customs & Funerary Etiquette for Modern Pagans,"* and I was desperately looking for a Heathen as passionate about death as I am to pepper with questions. A mutual friend had introduced us, knowing that Lea was also a mortician, and I suppose the rest is history, but her style, writing, and love for the gods to whom she is devoted impressed me so very much. We were fast friends, and ultimately, I came to rely on her for feedback, content, and camaraderie during that project— and it most assuredly would not be the book it is today without her involvement. All that aside, I could not possibly have anticipated the strangeness and magic that Lea would bring into my life. Loki, it seems, delights in seeking out anyone close to her and making himself known. My best example of this is the time Loki decided to ask me to buy her a wedding ring.

Yule of 2020 was approaching, and I'd planned to send Lea a care package. Loki made it known right away that he had a particular kind of gift in mind, and that nothing else would do. He wanted a ring for Lea, but not just any ring, oh no. He wanted an artifact, an ancient symbol of oaths representing all she was to him, and him to her. Here I was, righteously indignant at the prospect when weighed against the content of my wallet, and so I said no. Loki, of course, was having zero percent of this, bugging me and bugging me and bugging me. Endlessly showing up in dreams, everything I saw on the internet was rings, every commercial, whatever he could do to put that idea in front of me.

Then one day, there it was.

I was perusing a site I'd never been to before when I stumbled upon a sale including one tenth-century Viking era bronze "wedding ring" featuring a battered engraving that the listing called "Loki's Mask." I hesitated. It was too much—I truly couldn't afford it—and I said so, aloud. The response to that was an email notification, alerting me to an order from my website with a total that was exactly enough. To the penny, that order contained the cost of the ring, plus shipping.

How could I say no? I ordered the ring.

By the time I told Lea her gift would likely be late, and what it was, it was said over vacillations between "oh my god," tears, and laughter. I warned her that it being an antique made of bronze that if she wore it, it was likely to turn her finger green—and more laughter was had. At the time, I told her I hoped it fit at all, as being an antique it wasn't as though it came in a common size. She joked that it would likely arrive on her doorstep on the day she turned in the manuscript for the book you are reading now.

It did; and it did. What it did not do was turn her finger green.

— ◆ —

Truly, I cannot imagine anyone more lovingly devoted to Loki and Sigyn to tell their story, to dispel misconception, and to give them the devotional credit that they deserve. In all of the time that I've known Lea she has been an example of the love and joy that Loki can bring into the lives of those devoted to them, and Lea spreads that joy and laughter to all those around her. If my words could have any impact here at all, it would be to ask that you take a moment to allow that joy into your own life—if only through the reading of this book.

—Mortellus

INTRODUCTION:
THE STORY BEHIND THESE STORIES

To say Loki and Sigyn have had a tumultuous relationship with American heathens is like saying fainting goats are adorable: obvious, but criminally understated. New heathens looking for advice on working with Loki are often disheartened because of the dramatic discord and conflicting opinions, and in the case of Sigyn, there's hardly even any information at all. As a generational heathen oathed to Loki, he and his bride have been quite active in my life as of late, nagging and pulling strings to convince me to write this devotional. I did so gladly as a gift to Loki and Sigyn and as a gift to the heathen community. They deserve to have their stories shared, and the community deserves to learn more about them. We are, after all, a bunch of book nerds who love nothing more than research and academic debate. This book endeavors to satisfy both of those hobbies: to teach things you may not have considered (who's ready for a little etymology?!) as well as splash a little fuel onto the fiery controversy that surrounds The Trickster.

Loki has been a part of my life from my earliest memories onward, even when I didn't realize it. He's had some influence on my paternal grandfather, as well, a true OG heathen. Grandpa Frank Svendsen was born and raised in Norway and emigrated to NYC with his family in the last days of 1929, right when the world economy was starting to crumble. It's no small coincidence in my mind that the man I associate so strongly with Loki sailed to a new world in the midst of rising global chaos, even if he sailed on the *Stavangerfjord* and not Naglfar. He (and at least one of his brothers) was a proud heathen, and when my French Canadian/Italian Catholic mother met him as things got serious with my father—his son—she was utterly charmed by his humor and stories of the old ways. So she instilled in her daughter a love for the Nordic worldview, folklore, and mythology.

My father was heathen as well, but of the "unchurched" variety. There were no rituals or religious practices in our home, just the understanding that the old gods were real and, being a military household (in West Germany! Yes, I'm *that* old. I grew up on the front lines of the Cold War, baby!), entry to Valhalla was the ultimate goal. I grew up heathen, so when I reached those rebellious teen years, my big revolt involved converting to Catholicism. Upon our return to the United States, my mother enrolled me in Catholic school, partly for the quality of education, and partly so I could learn about Abrahamic philosophy. I'd grown up *completely* ignorant of Christianity and Mom knew I needed to learn about the Bible and the religions that sprang from it in order to understand other people in American society (I had, after all, had a pretty unconventional upbringing, and grew up overseas no less). Christian belief and thought are incredibly pervasive in this country, and I was oblivious to all of it.

At some point I caved to peer pressure and converted. Granted, it wasn't so much "wanting to fit in" as it was "wanting to partake in snack time at Mass;" regardless of the reason, it gave me a taste of belonging to a spiritual community and structured rituals. One of my high school memories involves a group of us gathered at lunch in an unofficial competition to see who had the weirdest family. I won (at least, that's how I remember it) with the commentary about my grandfather. "He still worships the 'old gods,'" I snickered to a group of uniformed classmates. "He even has little statue things of them in his bedroom!" Such heresy was practically unheard of in the mid-1990s, and the deviancy was all the more shocking by the fact it was a *grandparent* partaking in such nonsense rather than an edgy teen.

Another small bit of irony: my Catholic high school's mascot? The Vikings! The principal adored me for my surname. "Svendsen!" he'd cry in the halls. "There's our actual Viking!"

"Hail Óðinn!" I'd shout in response.

"Stop that! Don't let any of the priests hear you!" he'd hiss.

Even when I was experimenting with Christianity, I was always obnoxiously heathen, or at least talking about the gods. That habit has only gotten worse with age. It's now been over 20 years since I reverted back to my roots, and I seem to get more and more devout and intense with each passing year. Personal and spiritual growth is addictive, and once you get a taste of it there's no turning back. Besides, my brief run as a Catholic taught me the value of community, the comfort of ritual, and the draw toward monastic life. I'm grateful for having experienced Christianity because it actually made me a better heathen.

Incidentally, it also gave me the foundation for my career as a funeral director and embalmer, but that's another story altogether. Suffice it to say that my mom's decision to send me to Catholic school was key in giving shape to the kind of heathen I am today. I'm sure no one ever expected me to morph into a Lokean nun complete with veils (least of all myself), but here we are. If there's anything I've learned in life, it's that it never goes as expected. Best laid plans, and all that.

I said all of that to say this: this book is a work of devotion and love for Loki and Sigyn. I've known Loki almost all my life, and whenever I remember my grandfather, Loki is hovering at the edges. With Loki comes Sigyn, and her influence is quieter than her husband's, but just as intense, just as important. When I was in college at the turn of the century, I discovered that other pagans in the United States honored the Northern gods (yay!) and was horrified to learn of their disdain and distrust of the Trickster (oh NO!).

I mentioned it to Mom on a visit home, and she told me that's what she meant when she decided to send me to parochial school so I could learn how the rest of American society thinks. I didn't grow up under the influence of a faith that espoused dichotomous thinking, a concept so deeply ingrained that when people converted to polytheism, they subconsciously needed to assign a figure of evil to balance out the gods. She wanted me to learn and understand it so when I eventually did meet other heathens, I wouldn't turn my back on Loki. She's a neat lady, my Mom. I'm not saying she wanted me to learn about Christianity specifically so I wouldn't think Loki was evil. Rather, she wanted me to learn how others were raised so that I wouldn't question myself too harshly when I was released into the world.

The last few years have brought about some enormous advancements for Loki in the American heathen community, most notably the reversal of The Troth's Loki Ban at the end of 2018. Even in my own region, there's been a shift in the attitude toward the Mischief Maker, and I've used the reputation I and other Lokeans have built in that community to start getting vocal about why he's worth having around. It's been a genuine delight seeing stances soften as my friends and fellow heathens examine their biases and unpack the baggage they have regarding him.

I've also been sneaking Sigyn back into community consciousness. She's a treasure that the community has overlooked and forgotten for too long, and now more than ever we need the lessons and influence she brings. To my dismay, there's very little literature about Sigyn, and the scant bit that has been published has some questionable UPG (Unsubstantiated Personal Gnosis, or knowledge/understanding about metaphysical matters that aren't referenced in lore or history. For example, a lot of people associate foxes with Loki despite the fact foxes really aren't mentioned or represented anywhere in the archaeological record!).

It's a tremendous privilege to have this opportunity before me, to write a devotional for Loki and Sigyn for those who wish to learn about them. I pray that I honor them well as I share with you a bit of American heathen history and experience from the perspective of someone who grew up with these gods in a family that has honored them for several generations.

Loki and Sigyn are my greatest loves, and everything I do is for them. May these pages inspire you as the gods have inspired me.

HOW TO USE THIS BOOK

The tales covered in the first chapter are taken from the Poetic (or Elder) Edda and the Prose (or Younger) Edda. These are the primary sources for Scandinavian mythology, and they do double duty as handbooks for composing skaldic poetry by offering lists of common kennings (or descriptive phrases used instead of a noun, such as "leafy isle" in place of "tree") and advice for getting the meter just right. The poems that will be referenced most frequently include the *Völuspá*, or The Prophecy of the Seeress, in which Óðinn learns the history and fates of all gods and humanity, and the *Lokasenna*, or the Flyting of Loki.

Much to my editor's chagrin, there's quite a lot of "snark and backtalk" to be found here. To that I say: it's Loki's fault. Based on the sarcasm and commentary academics *also* fall victim to when writing scholarly research papers about Loki, I'm pretty sure it's literally impossible to write about the twerp in any other tone. It feels like there's some kind of cosmic rule at play here, so I do apologize for the tone of the first half of this book. I'm sorry, but I am simply bound by the laws of metaphysics here. Besides, the Northern gods are absurd, and their stories are even more absurd. It's why we love them so!

In respecting other people's experience and feelings, it's important to understand why Loki may not be a welcome figure at someone else's blót. As such, I spoke with heathens and pagans who fall on various points along the Loki/Noki spectrum. The thoughts and feelings of those who dislike and avoid Loki are included because their experiences are just as valid as those who enjoy having a little mischief in their lives. I hope these thoughts offer context to facilitate understanding and respect between Loki-folk and Noki-folk. After all, many of us aren't honoring every single god and goddess in the pantheon—just as with the humans around us, some of us jive better with some deities than with others. It would do Loki a grave disservice if I ignored those who try to ignore him. A community needs diversity to grow, and I sincerely pray that both sides reading this book come away with a better appreciation for differing points of view and more constructive conversations can take place for bettering the relationships between the Yay!Loki and Nay!Loki factions.

Because this book isn't exclusively for heathens, I describe basic heathen beliefs and practices to offer context for the culture surrounding Loki, Sigyn, and their Friends. A little bit of hospitality goes a long way, and the easiest way to offer hospitality to the divine is doing something for them within the cultural framework to which they are accustomed.

The Norse heathen ways of performing ritual or celebration tend to follow a pretty standard framework, so the sample rituals offered at the end of this book may be used as templates for customizing an offering or rite to the purpose or goal of your choosing. The blóts and meditations I've shared are actual rituals I have written, led, and performed to very positive reception all around. You may use them as written, or you may use the framework provided and use the kennings and intentions you wish to celebrate.

ABOUT THOSE FUNNY-LOOKING LETTERS

You'll notice I *generally* use common Anglicized spellings for names throughout the book with one glaring exception: Óðinn. I've always used the "Odhinn" spelling myself. I've been heathen since the dark ages of US English keyboards, when adding accents and special characters practically required a minor in coding. While writing this book, a linguist suggested I use the common Anglicized spelling for a wider audience and greater consistency with the rest of the terms and spellings used.

So I did. I shouldn't have. He didn't just let *me* know this was unacceptable, he made it clear to several people simultaneously that his name *must* be spelled "Óðinn."

You and I know that "Odin" would have worked just fine. A friend pointed out he *did* sacrifice himself for the runes, which are first and foremost an alphabet, so he gets a pass to dictate how his name is spelled. I'm a chipper idiot, but I'm not foolish enough to fight the Allfather (well, not this time anyway). So Óðinn it is.

All other names will appear in more familiar forms: Thor, Utgard-Loki, Vafthruthnir, etc. because they're what we're accustomed to in the English-speaking realm. I want this book to be an enjoyable read, not an eye-strain inducing jumble of Þórr, Útgarðaloki, and Vafþrúðnir. But Óðinn's gotta Óðinn. (Oh, and Skaði also gets the Eth because she kind of scares me and I can't bring myself to spell her name "Skadhi" when writing about her role in Loki's mythos.)

Whether you spell it Óðinn, Odhinn, Othan, Wotan, or Odin, that's between you and him. There's no wrong way as long as you're approaching him with sincere intent. But I'm not taking any chances here, so if he demands Óðinn, then Óðinn it shall be.

1
LOKI AND SIGYN IN THE LORE

Mischief Maker. Bringer of Gifts. Lie-Smith. Truth Teller. Sly One. Sigyn's Worry. Sigyn's Joy. Himself.

Like the rest of the Northern gods, Loki Laufeyjarson is many things to many people, and all things to some people. He's a liminal being, one of the more complicated and divisive creatures flitting about. In the stories of old, he's responsible for gifting the gods with their greatest treasures, but he's also responsible for their downfall and destruction. He's descended from giants, an honorary Ás (singular form of Æsir, the tribe of deities who live in realm Asgard), bound to Óðinn by oath of blood brotherhood, assigned the role of demon or devil by Christians during the conversion of Scandinavia.

He's hotly debated in heathen communities among those who see him as an evil figure and others who feel that he is one of the more compassionate and loving of the Northern gods. He's a Trickster, a Shapeshifter, a father and a mother both. He fulfills whatever role that's required, does what's needed, and faces the consequences each and every time. He's a source of laughter, hard truth, and more than a bit of chaos.

In short, he's a twerp.

— • —

The nature of mythology and lore is fluid. The stories are esoteric history that happened eons ago while still playing out in the present time. They're campfire tales our ancestors told one another to while away the long, frigid nights. Legends and truth, divine inspiration and human entertainment: they're the stories we share to keep the gods alive.

The old stories of the Northern people wouldn't be half as exciting or as hilarious if not for Loki. He's the driving force in many of the myths; he creates the conflict and then turns around and resolves it. He doesn't always do so happily, but he still takes responsibility and does what needs doing to resolve the problems he's created. The Sly One is the go-to for resolution even when he's not responsible for the initial trouble. His silver tongue is a force to be reckoned with, and his antics can certainly rub people the wrong way.

Scandinavian mythology is not a guide for morality in the way of Abrahamic lore. The God of the latter is an omniscient, omnipotent force of great, infallible power, and his word is law. The gods and goddesses of the Norse pantheon are flawed beings, every last one of them, and they endure hardships and trials and the threat of mortality. As such, their stories are just that: stories. The Eddas aren't a blueprint for how to live a god-honoring life. That's actually a relief when it comes down to it, because there's quite a lot of events and relationships that probably shouldn't be emulated in modern human society.

That said, Loki's characterization and antics in the myths make some folks uneasy. Some of his actions are viewed as violent, deplorable, and unnecessarily aggressive when viewed in isolation. Others examine his behavior within the context of the wider body of work comprising the lore and they see patterns of actions and reactions. This latter view doesn't necessarily excuse some of the things Loki does, but rather paints a broader picture of how all of the beings in the lore interact with one another and the consequences of those interactions. There are a *lot* of shady beings lurking around Asgard. Depending on who you talk to, Loki isn't always the worst of the lot (hi, have you met Óðinn yet? Sneaky old crank, that one).

Mythic society is a different beast than what we know and experience today. It's a foreign realm existing in a place outside of time as we know it, so reading the lore is best done without our own perceptions of what constitutes "good behavior." The people who first told these tales framed them within the context of their own society, which makes them tricky to adapt to our modern American culture. The best way to approach the myths is to recognize them as a product of their time and their people. There are eternal, universal values and ideas that transcend the millenia between the first storytellers and us today, but the lore is ultimately just a collection of rousing good fun, meant to entertain and to keep the gods alive in our minds.

And boy, do these gods and goddesses know how to entertain…

LOKI, THE KNOTTY GOD

We all know the power a name can hold. How many of us have looked up the meanings of our own names? How many expectant parents debate possible names based on what they represent? The power of names in mythology and folklore is even greater in those we humans use. Those names often offer insight into the personality, abilities, or attributes of the character in question. So what does Loki's name tell us about him?

Knot much, really.

You see, scholars don't think Loki's name really means anything, at least not anything specific that can be pinned down. There doesn't seem to be any attested use of his name in relation to the etymological origins in any of the lore or written history. Etymologist Anatoly Liberman has conducted extensive research on several words across Proto Indo European languages that could theoretically be linked to the origin of the name Loki.[1] While he offers discussions on words like *lokke/lokka/locke* (all Scandinavian words for "spider") and the Gaulish word *lugos*, or "raven" (parallel to the Raven trickster figure found in Indiginous folklore in North America), Liberman suggests *lúka* is the most likely origin or link.

In this context, the Icelandic verb *lúka* is translated as "to end or to finish."[2] Seems to be a suitable sentiment for a god

---

1. Liberman, Anatoly. 1994. "Snorri and Saxo on Útgarðaloki, with Notes on Loki Laufeyjarson's Character, Career, and Name." in *Word Heath = Wortheide = Orðheiði : Essays on Germanic Literature and Usage (1972-1992)*. Episteme Dell'Antichità E Oltre. Rome: Editrice il Calamo: 176–234.

2. Kevin French, message to author, April 1, 2021.

who has, for better or for worse, become synonymous with Ragnarok. Ragnarok—the Fate of the Gods—can be considered the heathen take on the apocalypse, though it's considerably more complex than that. It's not so much the end of all things as it is the ending of one cycle and beginning of another. But it's certainly an end to the majority of the gods and beings in Scandinavian mythology. *Lúka* is undoubtedly seatmates with the name Loki on that train of thought.

Lúka is also linked to an Icelandic word meaning "knot," which lends to one of the most common interpretations of Loki's name. Writer and professor of Old Norse Studies Eldar Heide has published articles regarding cultural relics and Loki's name in Icelandic language. Tradition holds that when working with fiber, knots in the thread are called *loki*. There's even a saying linking Loki the god with *loki* the tangle: "if one licks the end of a thread in order to thread a needle, one 'licks Loki's backside.'"[3] Thank goodness mortuary needles have eyelets that are large enough to thread the suture without licking the end because that would just make things a little weird when I'm embalming, eh?

Loki's mother is most commonly known as Laufey, hence his surname. However, she's sometimes called Nál. The Prose Edda actually refers to her as "Laufey or Nál" in both the *Gylfaginning* and the *Skáldskaparmál*. This name is the Old Norse and Icelandic word for "needle"! Thinking of Loki as the tangled thread and his mother as the needle makes his name,

---

3. Heide, Eldar. 2009. "More Inroads to Pre-Christian Notions, After All? The Potential of Late Evidence." In Á Austrvega: Saga and East Scandinavia: Preprint Papers of the 14th International Saga Conference.

Loki Laufeyjarson, all the more poetic, don't you think? Personally, it feeds the reputation he has in my mind for being a bit of a mama's boy.

The linguistic connection to knots is fairly apt considering Loki is credited with inventing the fishing net, which is just a series of knots along a collection of strings when you think about it. It also serves as allegory for his role in many of the myths as he's the one who tends to create a snarl in everyone else's plans. Think you're just going to wake up to have a nice, normal, quiet day? Sorry, Loki shaved your head while you were sleeping, so have fun absorbing that shock.

It's possible that Loki's name originally evolved from *lúka* but later became linked to knots because when a knot tangles a thread, you sometimes have to cut the thread and pick up with a *new* length cut from the spool. Hence referring to the tangled bit as a *loki*. We can imagine that Loki's name was intended to evoke "one who ends" and the knotty bit came later, in reference to ending the usefulness of the thread that has snarled. Anatoly Liberman reminds us that we will likely never pinpoint a specific meaning for the original meaning or origin of Loki's name.[4] Many have tried, and many have failed, because if there's anything that's going to be impossible to pin down, it's going to be the Trickster.

---

4. Liberman, Anatoly. 1994. "Snorri and Saxo on Útgarðaloki, with Notes on Loki Laufeyjarson's Character, Career, and Name." in *Word Heath = Wortheide = Orðheiði : Essays on Germanic Literature and Usage (1972–1992)*. Episteme Dell'Antichità E Oltre. Rome: Editrice il Calamo: 209.

FROM WHENCE HE CAME

We don't know much about Loki's parents beyond their names. In the Prose Edda, the *Gylfaginning* identifies his father as the giant Farbauti (or "Cruel Striker") and his mother as Laufey/Nál. There's nothing in the lore that definitively clarifies whether Laufey is a giantess or a goddess or something else entirely, which is curious considering Loki takes her name rather than his father's as one would expect in a patronymic society. That said, she *is* referenced in a little addendum Snorri Sturluson included in the Prose Edda: at the end of the *Skáldskaparmál*, there's a lovely series of skaldic verse that offers most of the kennings and metaphors we associate with the gods and other beings.

Not all copies of the Prose Edda have the addendum to the addendum, but scholars suspect a piece called the *Nafnaþulur*, in which Laufey is referenced, was a late addition tacked on after Snorri's time. In one of the thulur (Anglicized form of þulur, or poems that are more or less a list of names), Laufey's name is listed among the goddesses.[5] This seems to be the only clue we might have as to her nature, and could possibly explain why Loki's surname is Laufeyjarson and not Farbautason: Loki, being the liminal, world-straddling little sneak that he is, is both a giant and one who is counted among the Æsir in the *Gylfaginning*. If Laufey is one of the Ásynjur (goddesses of Asgard), it makes perfect sense for Loki to adopt her name when he's integrated into Asgardian society. By downplaying his Jotun roots

---

5. Lindow, John. 2002. *Norse Mythology: A Guide to Gods, Heroes, Rituals, and Beliefs.* Oxford University Press.

and highlighting his mother's side of the family, it's easier for him to get up to his hijinx among the gods.

I grew up associating her name with "Leafy Isle," which is a kenning (metaphorical name) for "tree." The relationship between Farbauti and Laufey is one of the links forming the connection with Loki's contested association to fire; Farbauti's "cruel, sudden strike" could be a nod to lightning. After all, fire tends to spring up when lightning strikes trees. Can't help but wonder if that's the Jotun version of The Talk when curious little giantlings ask about it. "Son, when a hot, strong bolt of lightning sees a nice, tall tree, her leaves swaying seductively in the wind, he just can't help but be drawn to her. Sparks fly, and that's where *you* come from!" Birds and the bees, lightning and the tree.

Weird thought, right? Buckle in, we're barely getting started.

So from Farbauti and Laufey's hot, hot heat came a bouncing bundle of baby Loki (aka Lopt) and his brothers Byleist and Helblinde. And thus ends what we know about Loki's lineage according to the Prose and Poetic Eddas.

FAMILY MAN

If nothing else Loki is a prolific parent, and his six children are as well known as Óðinn, Thor, and the Trickster himself. Of course, he's so into parenthood he's not just a proud papa, he's a proud mama as well.

Motherhood was bestowed upon Loki early in the mythology. In the creation myths, once Asgard is built the gods realize they need a massive wall to protect their realm. A contractor (likely a giant in disguise) wanders up to Asgard and offers to build their dream fortifications. Alas, the Æsir are pretty skint and instead of paying the giant outright, they agree to play a wager made by the not-so-giant giant: build the wall specifications in three seasons, and payment will be taken in the form of the sun and the moon … and Freyja's hand in marriage.

Freyja, Goddess of Love and Beauty, Queen of the Valkyries, Patron of Standing Up For Yourself When Men Try to Give You Away to a Contractor Who Might Be a Giant, lost her everlovin' mind at the gods for even *considering* these terms.

Loki proposed a counter offer: build the wall to our specifications in *one* winter—just you and your horse and no other assistance—and you get everything you asked for (probably muttering, "and be careful what you ask for" under his breath as Freyja continued hissing and spitting fury in the background).

The giant and his mighty stallion Svadilfari were on pace to win the bet. I wonder what the gods thought was worse: the prospect of losing their source of light and heat, or Freyja unleashing her unforgiving rage upon them before being dragged away to be a giant's hausfrau. Either way, they were on the fast track to prolonged misery and doom. The gods panicked and took out their frustrations on Loki for coming up with such a hare-brained scheme, then demanded he save them from their idiotic fate.

So Loki did. He saved their hides by shapeshifting into a mare and luring Svadilfari away on the last day before the final stones were set into place. Long story short, when Loki eventually returned to Asgard, he had with him a foal which he himself had birthed.

Let's all pause to imagine the moment Loki presents Sleipnir to Óðinn, beaming with pride. Everyone assembled looks on in horrified silence, asking themselves questions they really don't want answers to, as they watch young Sleipnir skitter-trot around Asgard on eight wobbly legs. "I made him," Loki gloats, a hand resting lightly against his belly.

And scene.

Next up in Loki's prolific progeny are the three he fathered with Angrboda, the giantess who rules over the forest of Ironwood in Jotunheim. Angrboda is a queen, making Loki her consort. They consorted quite a bit, and unto them were born Jörmungandr, Fenrir, and Hel. The other gods of Asgard were rather alarmed at Loki's progeny, especially Óðinn as he was privy to their role in the End Times thanks to the Seeress (as recounted in the *Völuspá* in the Poetic Edda). The Allfather took these three from the Father of Monsters and put them into safekeeping. Jörmungandr, the giant serpent, was cast out into the ocean where he encircled Midgard; Fenrir, the giant wolf destined to slay Óðinn, was tricked into bondage at the cost of the god Tyr's hand; and Hel, half woman, half corpse, was given domain over Helheim. Jormie and Hel definitely got the better deals here: Jörmungandr lives his best snakey life encircling the earth and has snakey children of his own, and Hel is a revered goddess of the dead who provides a quiet respite for those who die of old age, illness, and those who aren't shuffled off to the halls of one of the gods after death.

Fenrir, on the other hand … puns aside, he always had my sympathy as a child. As I matured, I understood why Óðinn had him tied up so that he couldn't harm anyone (or eat *him* in particular), but he remains a complex figure in the lore and in modern practice. Sure, the Seeress told Óðinn that he would be killed by the wolf at the end times, so Ol' One-Eye was taking precautionary measures to save his own hide. This action is probably what set Fenrir's fury into motion, however—who's to say if he would have been so keen on eating Óðinn upon his release if he *hadn't* been tied up and abandoned in the first place? That's the problem with knowing too much about what the future holds: in trying to avoid our fates, we set the very wheels in motion that seal the prophecy. Remember this. It's a recurring theme in Norse mythology.

As sympathetic as some of us may be to the way Loki and Angrboda's children were treated, pretty much everyone can agree on this: what happened to the sons Loki had with Sigyn is beyond the pale. As terrible as I felt for Fenrir as a child, it's nothing compared to the horror I felt (and still feel) about Narvi (also spelled Narfi, and sometimes Nari. I will use Narvi from this point on to avoid confusion with Narfi, the Jotun father of Nott/night) and Vali. As far as we can tell, these boys are pretty normal in appearance. At the end of *Lokasenna*, the tale in which Loki crashes a party in a peaceful hall, kills a servant, and then barges back in after being thrown out to call all the gods and goddesses out on their own faults and failings, the gods set upon him his punishment. They didn't *just* bind him to rocks in a cave with a venomous serpent suspended above his head. That bit is pretty understandable and justified, as a whole. It's *how* they bound Loki to the rocks that really devastates readers of the myth.

The gods turned Vali into a wolf and set him upon Narvi, killing him. What happened to Vali afterward is never mentioned, but poor Narvi's entrails are pulled from his body and used to tie Loki to the rocks.

And people wonder why Loki turned against the gods at Ragnarok.

As a Lokean, people have often asked me how I reconcile my adoration of Loki with his role in the death of the gods. I don't condone his actions at the end of the world as described in the lore, the way the myths present the war, but I certainly understand *why* he snapped and sailed Naglfar (the ship said to be made of dead men's fingernails) into Asgard. Loki might have been overreacting a tad if he'd simply been bound to the rock with regular chains, but to be tied up with the intestines of your murdered son? That's adding a *horrifying* element of extreme psychological torture to the punishment.

Loki may come off as a bit sociopathic in some of the myths, but in practice it's evident that he loves his children. The grief he feels at the treatment of most of his brood is heavy. There's some solace and pride in the reverence and honoring of Hel, but even so, his heart is heavy where his children are concerned.

WOULD YOU KNOW MORE?

When it comes to relaying the myths and tales involving Loki, well, there's no shortage of material. He's present in most of the tales and poems comprising the Prose and Poetic Eddas, serving as the pivot on which the action hinges (as well as providing the bawdy humor that kept the audience laughing through the long winter nights). When regarding these stories, it's helpful to bear in mind that they were spun and shared in a time and place when family blood feuds were more common than you'd think (even Snorri Sturluson, the Icelandic historian and poet who actually compiled the myths into the Prose Edda, was embroiled in a clan war against his own nephew). Modern societal mores and norms are quite far removed from the cultural and familial dynamics of that era.

It's also worth remembering that these come from oral tradition and are fairly dramatic; it's evident in the way many skaldic poems are written that they were intended to be performed with one or more speakers. As such, some of the action in the following tales is *absolutely* designed to get a reaction from a group of mead-drunk pagans.

Sif's Hair and the Gifts

The story about Sif's hair is one of the first laid out in the mythology, and for good reason: this is the tale explaining how the gods got their greatest treasures. And it's all because of Loki. Whether or not this is a good thing is open to interpretation.

There are many who are discomforted by Loki's cruel decision to cut Sif's glorious golden locks from her head. Thor sprang to his wife's defense in a rage and demanded Loki replace her hair and pay wereguild, or restitution. Our sneaky Trickster toddled off to the realm of the dwarves and set two smithing families against each other in competition for who could create the greatest tools for the Æsir. Well, he had one family make a wig of spun gold that would grow as hair once attached to Sif's head, and they took it upon themselves to make some fancy treasures for Óðinn and Freyr. Loki proclaimed them to be the very best smiths, which caught the attention of two brothers. Brokkr declared his brother could make Way Cooler Stuff, and Loki was all, "Game on! Loser forfeits his head!"

Turns out Brokkr's brother was making some Pretty Spiffy Things, and as Loki was fond of his head, he panicked and tried to throw the competition by turning into a fly and harassing Brokkr as he worked the bellows. This resulted in a bit of a botch-up in the making of Mjolnir, the famed hammer of Thor us heathens plaster everywhere as a sign of our faith. You see, war hammers had long handles for better leverage when swinging and smashing into skulls, but Loki's flying vermin antics resulted in Thor's hammer having a short, stubby handle (further commentary on such is left to the reader's own discretion).

Despite Mjolnir's defect, the gods were in awe and declared Brokkr and his brother to be the winners of the Competition of Magical Tools, Each One More Amazing Than the Last. Brokkr demanded Loki's head as his rightful trophy, which in a wry turn of legal eagle loophole exploitation, Loki agreed as long as Brokkr didn't remove any part of his neck in the process. After all, the loser's *head* was at stake, *not* the neck. The gods tore themselves away from admiring their shiny new pretties long enough to rule that Loki, Patron of Oily Lawyers, was correct.

Brokkr, outsmarted by Loki's silver tongue, shut him up by sewing his lips closed with an awl and leather string. And thus Loki gained the nickname Scar Lip.

Did We Learn Our Lesson?

This tale provides the origin of his kenning Bringer of Gifts. It's a bit of a roller coaster, starting with crappy behavior, accepting responsibility and making up for said crappy behavior, bringing some pretty amazing treasures to Óðinn, Thor, and Freyr, and then dipping back into shady nonsense and punishment. This is the general arc each of Loki's stories follows, but this one is particularly noteworthy of the gains for the gods.

Óðinn got Draupnir, the gold ring that drops eight more gold rings every nine days, and Gungir, the spear that never misses its mark when thrown. Freyr received Skíðblaðnir, a ship that always has favorable winds whether it sails by sea or sky and can fold down to pocket-sized portability, and Gullin-börsti, which as its name suggests, is a golden boar. And Thor not only restored his wife's boast-worthy locks with the golden hair transplant, but also gained the greatest treasure of all and the very symbol of the heathen faith, Mjolnir. Loki did a Nasty Thing by stealing Sif's hair, but hey, he did good on the weregild.

This is the myth that many use to exemplify Loki's bad side. There was no reason for him to rob Sif of her hair, which can be construed as an act of violence. It's a bit of a tricky story because on the one hand, this is how the gods receive their greatest treasures and weapons, but on the other … Yes, Loki is a creep in this one. One of the responsibilities we have as devotees to the gods is calling them out on unsavory behavior. If we don't hold *them* accountable, how can we possibly hold *ourselves* accountable?

Idunn's Terrible Adventure (or The Goat's Worst Day in Recent Memory)

The tale of Idunn's kidnapping is another story that's all over the place, starting out fairly innocently, but Loki does something stupid, then has to own up to his misdeeds and set things right.

It's a bit of a doozy, but all in all, I think the goat got the worst part of the deal throughout the whole thing.

Long story short, Loki thought a giant magic eagle overstepped his bounds when he was out and about with Óðinn and another god called Hoenir. In anger, he thwacked the eagle with a stick. Eagle took off and grabbed the stick in his talons. Instead of letting go, Loki-the-dope clung to the stick in terror. Turned out the eagle was none other than the giant Thjazi in disguise, and he refused to let Loki go unless he promised to bring to him the goddess Idunn and her golden apples of immortality. Loki swore the oath, and he was returned to Óðinn and Hoenir.

Upon their return to Asgard, Loki lured Idunn and her apples outside the wall surrounding their realm, and Thjazi— once again in eagle form—swooped in and snatched her. It didn't take long for the gods and goddesses to feel the absence of the immortality-granting apples, and when they realized Loki was the last one seen with her, they threatened him with death if he didn't get her—and her apples—back. Freyja even lent him her falcon cloak so he could fly to Thjazi's home in the mountains of Jotunheim with ease. Act of kindness or desperation for those apples? Either way, things ended badly for the soon-to-be-introduced goat.

In a rare stroke of luck, Idunn had been left alone for the day, so Loki shrank her down into a nut and flew off with Idunn-nut clutched in his talons. Thjazi returned home, saw her missing, and took off after Loki. The gods saw Loki-falcon approaching Asgard with Thjazi-eagle in hot pursuit, and once Loki crossed the border the rest of the gods set fire to a barrier of kindling outside the wall and killed Thjazi in the flames.

Shortly after, Thjazi's daughter Skaði came to Asgard demanding wereguild for his murder. There were a number of demands that were met; we learn about foot fetishes and why the stars literally watch us at night. But the coup d'etat comes when she says if they can't make her laugh, she'll slay them all. Naturally, this is Loki's time to shine.

Enter the goat.

When an ice giantess is enraged over her father's untimely death and puts incredible pressure on everyone to make her crack a smile, there's not a lot of time to arrange a witty improv troupe or some ace delivery on a stand-up act. No, apparently when the heat gets this hot, Loki's recourse is to drop trou, tie his scrotum to a goat's beard, and play tug of war.

Ears were assaulted by the shrill squeals coming from both Loki and the poor goat. The goat was horrified. Loki was in agony. Everyone was traumatized. Everyone, that is, except for Skaði. When Loki couldn't bear the torment any longer, he collapsed in her lap and was regaled with her laughter at the ridiculousness of what she'd just witnessed. Great job, Loki, you saved everyone's lives by tying your balls to the beard of a panicked goat. Keeping it classy in Asgard.

Did We Learn Our Lesson?

Don't hit eagles with sticks. In fact, to be on the safe side, just don't hit *any* animals with sticks. Not cool, Loki. Not cool.

This is a story that didn't need to unfold in a riot of kidnapping, murder, or tormenting goats with risque bouts of tug-of-war. When Thjazi makes his offer to Loki about Idunn, Loki should have let Óðinn in on the situation. Together, they surely could have come up with a way to protect Idunn and avoid dragging other innocents into the mess. That's what friends are for—they help us when we're in a bad situation, and they help us brainstorm solutions that help more than they hurt. It's nice that Loki is a man of his word and follows through on a promise made in duress, and better that he rescued Idunn and satisfied Skaði's final requirement for restitution. But he'd have proven himself far more trustworthy if he'd just asked for help from his closest friend.

Feeling Pretty

Shapeshifting into a mare isn't the only time Loki dances along gender lines. Who doesn't know the tale of Thor dressing up as Freyja to reclaim his hammer, Mjolnir? It's a fun one, full of Loki being, well, Loki.

Once upon a time, the giant Thrym stole Mjolnir, which threw the gods into a bit of a panic. I'm not sure if you've picked up on how many times the gods panic, but it's a distinct running theme in the lore. After all, Mjolnir was their best defense against the giants. ("Cool, guys, guess the wall is meaningless? You know, the one I had to GIVE BIRTH for? Do you know the PAIN of delivering a horse with EIGHT sharp little hooves?!") Thrym agreed to give the hammer back in exchange for Freyja's hand in marriage. "OH HEL NO, NOT THIS AGAIN!" Freyja screamed. Cue running theme number two. Never fear, though—Heimdallr has a plan!

The Plan: dress Thor up to look like Freyja, and Loki will tag along dressed as her bridesmaid. Thor dislikes this plan. Freyja is okay with it. Loki's excited about it.

The plan's a go.

They do such a great job dressing Thor in Freyja's finery that none of the giants at Thrym's hall suspect a thing until Thor eats half of the food at the feast, then glares menacingly at Thrym. Loki is quick to cover for his bosom buddy, blithely assuring Thrym that Freyja had been fasting from sheer excitement and is mad with lust for their wedding night.

A beautiful, heart-touching wedding ceremony followed, during which Loki certainly shed a tear or two ("Always a bridesmaid, never a bride," he probably lamented under his breath, so swept away with emotion was he). Thrym called for Mjolnir to be placed in his bride's lap to hallow the union.

This is where we learn why just because something's Tradition, it doesn't have to be followed.

Once Mjolnir was laid in Thor's lap, he grabbed it and killed Thrym and everyone assembled, ruining his wedding gown—and his marriage—in the process. Loki's not exactly known for being a rage-fueled fighter like Thor, so there's no mention of what he did during the massacre. Probably just twirled around in all of the blood raining down while dodging falling bodies, singing "I Feel Pretty" or something.

Did We Learn Our Lesson?

There's not a lot of commentary on this one. Just choose your traditions wisely, and sometimes you just have to feel pretty. It's okay to experiment with your style and try something new. Gender lines are a purely social construct, so blur them and decimate them and dance in the blood of the patriarchy!

Also, there's a caveat about being *too* pretty: take it from Freyja, it's not often as awesome as it seems. On the days I myself am feeling rather frumpy and uninspired, I say, "At least I'm not a constant pawn when bartering with skeevy giants."

Poor Freyja.

Let's Not *Meet Under the Mistletoe*

Baldr, son of Óðinn and Frigg, is supposed to be invincible but (and there's *always* a "but" in stories with Loki) is killed by a sprig of mistletoe. Whether or not Loki was responsible for the death itself is up for debate. There's also some mild confusion about whether the deadly mistletoe is the actual twiggy little plant or the name of a sword (after all, the Eddas were committed to writing in Iceland, where no mistletoe grows). Heathens love a good academic scuffle, so the conversations surrounding this particular myth are myriad. The more mead being consumed, the more animated and intense said discourse becomes.

This tale starts out as a testament to a mother's love. Frigg prophesied the death of her beloved Baldr, the Shining One, and demanded promises from all things that they would not harm him. Mistletoe, be it the plant or the sword, was overlooked. Remember, these stories are all set in a time and place without a whole lot of entertainment options, so the residents of Asgard took to amusing themselves by throwing stuff at Baldr. Axes, swords, arrows, rocks, probably a goat or two: nothing was more hilarious than trying to kill a being who couldn't die. I'm sure hucking dangerous things at an immortal is fun at first, but I'd imagine it gets pretty redundant after a while. I don't know about you, but I for one am glad to live in a world with books, movies, and the internet to while away my own down time.

In the Poetic Edda (aka the Elder Edda), the *Völuspá* indicates that Hod (Baldr's brother) alone slayed Baldr with mistletoe/Mistletoe. The Prose Edda (the Younger Edda) tells it differently. When Frigg beseeched all objects to grant her son immunity, Loki learned that she'd neglected to ask the young mistletoe plant its oath. When everyone else was living it up trying to strike Baldr down, Loki fashioned a spear or arrow out of the mistletoe, then cozied up to the blind Hod. "Feeling a little left out, are you? Pretty ableist of them, isn't it?" he purred. "Let me help you take part in some reindeer games." Loki put the missile-toe into Hod's hand, walked him up to the firing line, and guided Hod's aim and release. Baldr died, everyone cried.

Well, not *everyone.*

Loki may or may not have been involved in Baldr's death, but on this both the Poetic and Prose Eddas agree: Loki definitely made sure Baldr *stayed* dead.

A distraught Frigg begged Hel to release Baldr from her realm. Hel said she'd gladly do so if *everything* in existence, sentient or no, wept for Baldr. This time, Frigg was thorough in her request. All things wept for the lost Baldr, all things but one: a giantess refused to shed a single tear for Óðinn's son. The giantess isn't identified as Loki in the Prose Edda's version of the myth, but the Poetic Edda proves it. When Frigg and Loki get into it in the *Lokasenna,* he crows over the fact that *he's* the reason Baldr wasn't released from Helheim. Bold move, pipsqueak.

So, Loki may have been instrumental in Baldr's death, or he may not have been, but he *did* see to it that Baldr remained in the realm of the dead until after Ragnarok's conclusion. *This is where the debates can get mighty interesting.*

As established in the Poetic Edda's *Völuspá*, Óðinn knows that Ragnarok is the final war that will kill the gods and destroy the world as they know it. This is why he takes precautionary measures, such as binding Fenrir. Everything the Old Man does is designed to prevent (or at least postpone) the end of times. Yet the Seeress in the *Völuspá* doesn't end her prophecy with the death of the gods. Once the dust settles at the end of the war, she speaks of Baldr returning from the underworld, and he and the children of the other gods—the second generation, if you will—rebuild the world into a new and glorious utopia, ushering in a golden age for society.

The question that arises: Óðinn knows this. He knows Baldr survives Ragnarok because he was sheltered and safe in Helheim as the war raged in Asgard. He knows what Loki's role is in all of this. Even if Loki isn't instrumental in guiding Hod's hand to kill Baldr, he still leads the opposing forces at Ragnarok, kicking off the spree of death and destruction. Óðinn *knows* this and *he makes the oath of blood brotherhood with Loki anyway.* He *still* brings him into the Asgardian fold. Did he bring Loki on board as a brother because he needed Loki to ensure Baldr remains safe and sound in the realm of the dead despite Frigg's grief-fueled interventions?

Did We Learn Our Lesson?

Ultimately, if we try to avoid a certain outcome, we may well be setting into motion the very chain of events that will ensure the unwanted conclusion. Be careful with the knowledge you receive and try not to upset the order of nature.

And this goes without saying, but don't hurl sharp deadly things at people, even if they're supposed to be invincible. Get a real hobby. Rude.

Fire-Eater

One of the myths in which Loki doesn't act the fool is one which I find deeply fascinating. This story lays the foundation for an interesting idea regarding Loki's original nature and offers some insight as to why he's regarded as a fire god. Utgard-Loki's tale is a curious one, feeling a bit out of place among the rest of the myths. There doesn't seem to be much of a point to this one beyond simple entertainment, and it includes beings who represent abstract concepts within the story itself. It also, curiously, depicts giants as massively oversized beings that we tend to associate with, well, giants, whereas the rest of the use of "giants" is in reference to the race or tribe of beings known as Jotuns (of whom Loki is one, remember, and who many of the gods have married and/or produced children with). As far as we can tell in the rest of the stories, the Jotuns aren't much larger than the Æsir, Vanir, or humans of Midgard.

This tale involves beings so large that Thor and Loki sleep inside a giant's glove. Its scale is so massive they don't recognize it as an article of clothing. This detail seems innocuous but carries greater weight than one would imagine: sleeping in gloves is a sore subject for Thor as evidenced in both the *Lokasenna* and in another account of flyting found later in Poetic Edda, the *Hárbarðsljóð* (the best approximation I can offer regarding that pronunciation is to shove a potato into your mouth and sneeze). Both poems include wry comments about the time he slept in a glove, to which Thor responds with the rage of a heavily bruised ego. Word to the wise: don't leave any stray gloves on or around an altar set up for Thor.

In this story, Thor and Loki are traveling and exploring as they often do, and following a mishap with Thor's goats, Thor takes on a couple of human children as servants. Eventually, they reach their destination of Jotunheim and sneak into the castle home of Utgard-Loki. The homeowner and his guests are feasting, but graciously pause to mock Thor and Loki for being such wee little creatures. Challenges are issued in order to restore the Asgardians' pride, and naturally, our heroes fail each task because things aren't exactly as they seem in the castle.

Thor's very quick-footed boy servant lost his race with a fellow who turned out to be Thought (as in, the racing thoughts that speed through our minds that no man can ever hope to outrun); Thor failed to lift a cat off the ground because the cat turned out to be Jörmungandr the world serpent ("Hiya Dad!" he might have hissed with a giant snakey grin had his true form been revealed in Loki's presence; alas, Utgard-Loki didn't reveal the illusions until he was kicking his guests out the next day). And Loki? Loki lost an eating contest. And this is the interesting bit of the tale, as far as I'm concerned.

Loki is commonly depicted as being tall and lean, a significant juxtaposition against the broad, muscular, beefy Viking stereotype. He also has a voracious appetite, both evidenced in the myths (see: smacking a magic eagle with a stick for taking the best part of a roasted ox) and in the experiences modern day devotees have with him (one of the kennings a handful of us use in ritual to hail him includes "Raider of Fridges." There seems to be a running theme of people dreaming of him helping himself to the contents of their refrigerators while he chats with them, imparting whatever Wisdom or Lesson he thinks they need to hear). So lean and greedy suggests he has an enviable metabolism, and this story proves he can pack away more than anyone would ever expect in a very short amount of time. Loki Laufeyjarson: Speed Eater Extraordinaire.

So in this strange little story, Loki kicks off the series of Impossible Challenges by declaring no one can eat as quickly as him. This was a sly little boast on his part as he was famished from his travels and figured such a claim would give him full access to the feast on Utgard-Loki's tables. Spoiler alert: it worked. All hail the Scarfer of Other People's Food.

The contest was set against Logi; Loki and Logi took their positions at opposite ends of a meat-laden table and proceeded to devour everything along the table. The first to reach the middle would be declared the winner. Loki and Logi hit center at the same time, but Loki lost on a technicality. Loki stripped all of the bones of their meat cleanly and perfectly, sure enough. His opponent, however, not only consumed all of the meat, but the bones and the table itself. It's later revealed that Logi is none other than wildfire. And this is where things get a little esoteric.

Did We Learn Our Lesson?

This contest illustrates the difference between fire that rages uncontrolled and the purpose of fire used in ritual or sacred spaces. I've never acknowledged Loki in the images of forest fires or brush fires decimating landscapes in the dry season, but I've always felt him in the softly rumbling hiss of the cremation process. My experience as a mortician isn't limited to just the preparation room and embalming: I'm also a certified crematory operator. A strange little quirk of mine is to greet Loki upon seeing the flames of the afterburner when opening the retort to commit a body.

When enough time has elapsed, the retort is again opened to reveal all tissues have been consumed, leaving behind nothing but the inorganic bone matrix of the skeleton (that is, the mineral structure of the bones such as calcium and phosphorus). Cremation fire is sometimes regarded as being just as sacred as it is practical.

Consider again the contest between Loki and Logi. Loki consumed all of the meat but left the bones behind. Logi consumed *everything* in his path. Loki is regarded as a fire deity, and though this is a topic often debated, this particular tale reinforces the concept. The fire associated with Loki isn't *destructive* fire: he's a deity of *sacred* fire. Logi obliterated everything along the table, including the table itself, while Loki's flame is more like that of the cremation pyre. Of course, I'm not staking that claim just because I've always thought of Loki when cremating a body or because the Loki vs Logi story reminds me of cremation. In fact, I'm not the only one who's made the connection between Loki as sacred/cremation fire.

Dagulf Loptson, an author and noted Lokean in American heathenry, published an excellent two-part essay ("A New Place For Loki Pts. I & II") which is further fleshed out in her book, *Playing With Fire: An Exploration of Loki Laufeyjarson.*

She *also* suggests that the story of Loki vs Logi is an allegory for the difference between sacred fire and destructive fire, drawing the same parallel to cremation that I had during my years of mortuary work.

Her work further examines the notion of Loki as a fire god, suggesting through copious research the possibility of Loki representing the *sacred* fire in which offerings are burned while Sigyn represents the act of placing offerings into the flame. This idea resonates deeply with me while offering a possible explanation for the vitality of the modern day cult of Loki. Loptson muses that the Christianization of the myths represents the death of the Old Way: if Loki is sacred fire and Sigyn represents committing offerings to the flame as transport from Midgard to Asgard and Vanaheim, then the transformation of gifts/offerings to venom and the sacred flame to a reviled frith-breaker bound to a rock underground surely represents the poisoning of gifts and cutting off access to the old gods.[6] If we run with this idea, it may shed insight into the lack of a defined cult of Loki in the pre-Christian records and the rather large cult of Loki in modern practice.

Suppose Loki and Sigyn were integral deities to the act of ritual and offerings in the original practices. They would likely have been a part of most blóts, if only in the act of holding the offerings above the fire/committing the gifts to the fire. It could have been such an ingrained concept that there was no particular need to separate them out into distinct cults and regional

6. Loptson, Dagulf. 2014b. "A New Place for Loki, Part II." Polytheist.com. September 23, 2014. http://polytheist.com/orgrandr-lokean/2014/09/23 /a-new-place-for-loki-part-ii/.

practices. They would simply have been the means by which the gods, goddesses, and ancestors received the offerings which sustained them. Then Christianity comes along, and the gifts are turned to venom, the sacred fire demonized, and the gateway between our world and the pagan divine is effectively sealed shut. The old gods begin to hunger and wane. Centuries pass, and they're still alive in the hearts and minds of many through myths and stories and culture, but they need more. They need the energy that comes with offerings. They're *starving*.

And so Loki ventures out, searching for "food," because he was the one who always relayed it to the others. He was the portal, the Bringer of Gifts, and it's his duty to secure those gifts. So out he goes into the world, looking for sustenance, tapping and poking and prodding those who will listen. He makes himself known in the modern age, and his devotees are steadily rising in numbers. Now he has a defined cult, whereas he didn't have such a thing in the past as best we know. But he's loud these days, drumming up attention because the gods need humans to turn their energy and gifts to them again. They were starving, so Loki went looking for food. He found it. Once again, great numbers of heathens are giving food and offerings to the fire, gifting the gods with what they need so that we may get the inspiration and strength that we need in Midgard.

Are they doing it specifically because of Loki? No, and many of them will tell you that with dramatic emphasis. But I can't speak to the forces at play luring people into heathenry. I was raised this way, so I don't have a "Come to Óðinn" moment (or rather, "Come to Freyja" as it may be; seems like a disproportionate percentage of people I know in the community credit

Freyja with enticing them into the faith. Though, I admit, she *was* the one welcoming me back after my failed experiment with Christianity. Perhaps I'm too generous in my phrasing ... it wasn't so much a "welcome back" as the sensation of a bemused relative leaning in the doorway, smirking and saying, "Well, well, look what the cat dragged in. Yeah, how'd *that* work out for you?" It was a different sort of "prodigal child" moment, I suppose). I just kind of grew up taking the gods—and Loki—for granted. Who knows what was going on behind the scenes, who was tipping things over and moving pieces around to upset the order of what someone *thought* they knew, dismantling their knowledge of the spiritual world and leading them to a whole new worldview. Not my place to say, or to declare that Loki had any hand at all, no matter how slight, in the conversions of others. Doesn't mean I'm not going to be a bit of a twerp myself and plant that little seed of "wait ... " in the backs of people's minds.

Hey, I'm a Lokean. Did you really think I *wasn't* going to say something controversial to rile up the blood?

Flyting (When Loki Brings the Receipts ... Or Does He?)

Flyting is an Old English and Old Norse practice that has evolved to something like the modern rap battle: it's a spoken word exchange of insults, usually said in a poetic meter (or rhythm). The *Lokasenna* is also known as "The Flyting of Loki" because the bulk of it consists of Loki slinging barbed verses (in skaldic meter) at his victims. Whether or not this tale is accurate or heavily distorted by Christian judgement, it still offers some valuable insight.

Aegir is the god of the deep sea, the frightening, unpredictable bits beyond the safety of shallow shores. Despite the fear associated with such unexplored depths, his hall is a sanctuary some distance away from Asgard's lands: his rules declare that no fighting is allowed, period. Obviously, this means it's the perfect setting for Loki to go all out psycho and get Ragnarok a'rollin. The *Lokasenna* is one of the more jaw-dropping of the myths, and it's also one that's considered to have had a heavy dose of Christianized tampering by dear old Snorri. Some of the accusations made in the story sound as though they're based in Christian morality and at odds with the tone and events of the rest of the mythology. In fact, Lee Hollander's translation of the Prose Edda includes a note regarding the disparity between the *Lokasenna* and the rest of the lore. He warns that the claims made against the gods and goddesses assembled likely aren't accurate, nor is it likely that this particular flyting was originally a popular or canonical part of pre-Christian lore, so readers should approach the *Lokasenna* with caution.[7]

Once the shock of Baldr's death eased up, several of the gods and goddesses retreated to the sea god's hall to partake in ale and feasting. Loki was in a bit of a mood, apparently, because he bristled when someone praised one of Aegir's servants. Because we're talking about Loki, "bristled" means "killed the servant for no reason." This leads to his swift and rightful expulsion from the feast.

After stewing a bit, Loki forces his way back into Aegir's hall and demands a drink. He accuses Óðinn of breaking the blood

---

7. Hollander, Lee M. 1988. *The Poetic Edda.*

oath between them, during which the Allfather declared whenever a drink is offered to him, one must also be given to his brother Loki. Yet there the Old One-Eyed Bastard sat enjoying his ale while Loki stood without a drop to soothe his parched tongue. The attentive reader will pause at this moment and think, "Hm. Maybe he should stay parched, because something tells me Nothing Good will come from lubricating this guy's tongue." Óðinn bids his son Vidar to allow Loki to sit between them and to fill Loki's cup. Loki drinks, but he doesn't sit. The Mischief Maker is salty about being treated badly for so long, and he decides to call *everyone* assembled out on their secrets and lies.

This scandalous exposé goes on until Thor shows up. He's so enraged by what he's hearing he smashes his hammer around Aegir's hall. Loki flees, and the gods give chase.

Upon his capture, The Punishment begins: Loki's son Vali is turned into a wolf and kills his brother Narvi, the gods use Narvi's entrails to bind Loki to rocks, and Sigyn steps in to hold the bowl above his face to spare her husband the added agony of a serpent's venom burning his flesh. When she must step away to empty the bowl, the pain from the venom dripping onto his face causes him to writhe against his bonds, causing the earth to tremble and quake. When he is eventually freed, he will rally troops to join him in the war against the gods. So begins Ragnarok, and so ends the reign of the gods we've come to know in the mythic cycle.

Did We Learn Our Lesson?

While it's likely that Snorri Sturlson was being a good Christian by demonizing the pagan gods (while still preserving Iceland's cultural and literary history), he still gives us crumbs to play with. For instance, I suspect Loki was tired of always being picked on and mocked and called upon to get the gods out of sticky situations that weren't always of his making (as often as he *is* to blame, he *isn't* the only instigator throughout the lore). He plays the fool in many of the tales while everyone else pretends to be perfect and blameless. As my mom said when we were talking about the *Lokasenna* in the early Aughts, there's only so much someone can take before they snap.

In my practice, *Loki is a god of accountability.* Even when he does stupid things and has to untangle messes of his own making, he acknowledges his responsibility and follows up by correcting the situation to his victim's satisfaction. He's also a Forcer of Truth, demanding we cast away the masks we wear to placate society and own up to who we are at heart. The more you lie to others about yourself, the more you lie to *yourself*; the problems and vices you hide will never go away, and they're certainly not going to resolve themselves. If you don't admit to anything, you can't work on becoming better or creating a better situation for yourself and those around you. In order to improve as a person and as a valued member of society, you have to be able and willing to face the worst parts of yourself and overcome them rather than hide them and let them fester.

That said, the flyting in the *Lokasenna* is a curious read because not only are the insults suspiciously Christian in their morality, but the other gods and goddesses don't dispute *any* of them. Loki just goes around the room, accusing the others of being weak and cowardly, being promiscuous, engaging in incest, practicing sorcery, and crossing societal gender lines (particularly ragging on Óðinn for practicing witchcraft, which is apparently a girly thing to do?). It's a strange way to end a collection of stories that revel in the use of magic, dressing like the opposite gender or taking on the form and function of the opposite sex, and lots (and lots) of out-of-wedlock sex. *None* of these things were cast in any kind of moral judgement or derisive tone in the other myths, but suddenly they're presented as shameful, sinful behaviors in the flyting.

If this was doctored by Snorri, I'm pretty sure Loki had *way* better tea on the other gods and goddesses in the original form. Sleeping around and practicing magic are the *least* scandalous things that happened in the rest of the lore—sagas included—so it's kind of a weak attempt to demonize pagan gods. I'm sure it worked on the Christians of Snorri's time and validated their conversion away from such ill-behaved idols, but it falls a bit flat in the shadow of everything else we have in the Eddas, sagas, and skaldic poetry. Context matters.

Something to Ponder

When reading the lore, some curious thoughts may or may not creep into the base of your brain as you reflect on what we know about Óðinn and the prophecy laid out in the *Völuspá* and how the rest of the myths play out. Consider this: Óðinn knew more about how everything would play out that the *Völuspá* even lets on. He knows Loki's involvement in everything, and he decides to make Loki his right-hand man regardless via their oath. How much does Loki know about how events will unfold? Did Óðinn tell him anything of the Seeress's prophecy? Does Loki know what he's going to have to do? Does Óðinn share any detail, or a vague outline, giving Loki the choice to accept the responsibility of what's to come? Does Loki accept the role being offered to him out of a sense of necessity? It's a terrible burden to shoulder, but perhaps it was made easier as the gods turned against him as time went on.

No matter how you interpret it, Ragnarok isn't a fun time. But the barest glimmer of empathy certainly lends an understanding of why he ultimately leads an army into Asgard. Whether or not Óðinn knew exactly *how* the prophecy would play out, regardless of how much he may or may not have warned Loki in advance, you have to admit that Loki genuinely suffered for his actions. I would certainly hope that no one can justify the fact he was *bound in that cave with his murdered child's entrails*. Did he deserve his punishment? Probably. Even I can admit he took things too far in Aegir's hall in the *Lokasenna*. Did his children deserve their roles in that punishment? No! It was an extra measure of unbelievable cruelty, a step too far, an action far more horrifying than anything Loki ever did up to this point in the lore. Not that it gives him a free pass to destroy everyone and everything, but let's be honest: he had his reasons. He's a flawed, angry, relatable figure... *just like the rest of the Norse gods.*

It all comes down to your own understanding of and relationships with the gods. The myths are just that—stories. They help us understand the nature of the gods and their relationships among each other and the realms. They're merely guidelines and introductions to who they *really* are. It's up to *you* to get to know the gods better. Some of us get along with some deities and keep a wide berth from others. There can be mutual dislike based on experience and agenda. But really, it does more harm than good to point to the myths as though they are Gospel and say "This is who is good and this is who is evil, and these stories tell us why."

Like the Bible, those stories are filtered through the theological and political biases of the men who wrote them down centuries ago. They're a starting point for conversation, and it's up to you to take it deeper.

ABOUT THAT ASH LAD ...

Nothing ever seems to be simple where Loki is concerned. Believe it or not, there's actually debate in some corners of the community regarding Loki's status as a deity! I've actually heard people insist that he's nothing more than an overly glorified land spirit who shouldn't be venerated at the same level as the gods (or at all). We'll just ignore the whole "Loki is counted among the Æsir" bit in the Eddas then, eh?

It's easy to understand why this particular argument rumbles along. After all, there's no concrete archaeological or literary evidence of Loki having a cult of worship in pre-Christian Scandinavia. There are several "cultural artifacts" that indicate Loki was a known entity way back when, and some of them are conflated with folktales about the Ash Lad in Norway and Denmark. I myself have been a fan of Asbjørnsen and Moe's collection, *Norwegian Folktales,* since I received my first copy at age six (in fact, my first tattoo is taken from that book, an image I've called my Loki-fox since I first saw it). Ash Lad is a recurring character in the stories and there's a number of similarities between him and the Loki of mythic lore.

He's generally considered to be the youngest of a trio of brothers; we don't know if Loki is younger than Byleist and

Helblinde, but his behavior in the myths is often reminiscent enough of a petulant toddler (I love Loki, but facts are facts) that it's not terribly difficult to imagine. They're both outsiders who don't really, truly seem to belong with the company they keep. Ash Lad is the lazy mama's boy who lounges around the hearth all day; I've always suspected Loki's a bit of a mama's boy himself, not least of all because he took her name instead of his father's.

An archaeological find in Denmark known as the Snaptun Stone might be evidence of a Loki-Ash Lad connection. The Snaptun Stone is a hearth stone depicting the face of a man whose mouth is sewn shut. You'll recall that Loki's lips were sewn together by the dwarf Brokkr in the myth about the creation of Mjolnir. The carving on this hearth stone could be proof that Loki of the myths was venerated as a god, a rare relic acknowledging his presence in people's homes. That it's specifically a *hearth stone*—a stone laid in the front part of the floor of a fireplace—lends weight to the concept of Loki as a fire deity. It *also* suggests that Loki of the Eddas is a *version* of Ash Lad of the fairy tales. After all, Ash Lad got his name because of his lazy, layabout ways sitting around the hearth all day.

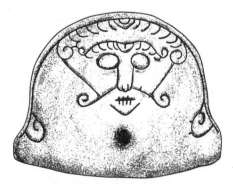

Snaptun Stone

In several tales of the Ash Lad, he's depicted as being the type who's voted "least likely to succeed," a scrawny little slip of a guy who isn't as strong or skilled as his brothers. He still manages to gain the upper hand time and again because of his quick wits and astounding creativity, and he sometimes manages to secure treasures for the odd king here and there. Starting to understand why some people think Ash Lad and Loki are one and the same?

Who knows? Maybe they are. Does that mean Loki's nothing more than a Nordic Paul Bunyan or Johnny Appleseed? Nope. He's obviously much more than a popular character in regional folklore. He's specifically counted among the Æsir in the Eddas, he's a primary figure in most of the mythology, and he wields greater abilities and influences among the other gods than a mere land spirit could hope to manage. Óðinn made an ancient oath with Loki, elevating him to stand as his brother and to live and travel with the Æsir regardless of his background. Personally, I think that Ash Lad is more likely to be evidence of Loki's popularity than evidence of his status as a spirit or fairy tale character. The Nordic countries converting to Christianity may have disrupted the popularity of the stories of the old gods, but Loki was entertaining enough to inspire more contemporary yarns as the Ash Lad.

Shapeshifters are sly and tricksy beings. The other gods were being relegated to the back burner, but perhaps Loki simply snuck his way into other tales and adventures throughout Scandinavian culture. Or maybe there's no connection, only coincidence. Either way, Loki is far too formidable a being to be written off as an over-inflated land spirit.

As I've said before, the lore and history are merely stories and ideas providing a foundation on which to build your practice. Your own experience with Loki—*whatever* he is in the great primordial scheme—will inform your own beliefs.

If nothing else, there's certainly one thing we can *all* agree on regarding Loki: he's infuriatingly complex, his motives are infuriatingly tricky to untangle, and he's at the root of a lot of infuriating arguments in the academic sphere as well as within the American heathen community. He's just infuriating.

Delightful, but infuriating.

SPECULATING ABOUT SIGYN

Sigyn is the Norse goddess of loyalty and compassion. We know her for her devotion to her husband, Loki: she holds a bowl to catch venom from the snake suspended above his bound form, sparing him the agony of feeling it drip into his eyes. This act reflects her dedication to shield us in Midgard from the poisons around us and her steady companionship so that we are never alone in our suffering. While her husband is known for stirring chaos and his loud mouth, Sigyn is the quiet comfort and compassionate heart taking care of those impacted by the forces of change. This is what we know of her from the lore.

She is one of the few goddesses specifically named in the Poetic Edda's *Völuspá* and she appears in the *Lokasenna*; in both cases, Sigyn is only mentioned in her role as Loki's wife, who holds the bowl above his face to catch the venom. Her name appears again in the *Skáldskaparmál* in the Prose Edda, used as a kenning to identify Loki, "Husband of Sigyn," and again at the end in the list of Ásynjur (goddesses). In the tenth-century Norwegian skaldic poem Haustlöng, she is again referenced in the form of Loki's kenning, this time as "The Burden of Sigyn's Arms." This isn't a direct reference to her role holding the bowl, however: "the burden of so-and-so's arms" is an oft-repeated kenning throughout the lore.

Beyond those poems and their counterparts in the Prose Edda, there is scant record of archaeological or historical cult worship of the goddess. She does have the distinction of appearing on the Gosforth Cross, a tenth-century stone monument in County Cumbria in England. The cross bears a number of carvings depicting various scenes from both Norse and Christian myths and stories; Sigyn is seen holding the bowl above the bound figure of her husband. This pose or a variant thereof is replicated again and again in the majority of artwork featuring her. The bowl is often the identifying symbol in images pertaining to Sigyn.

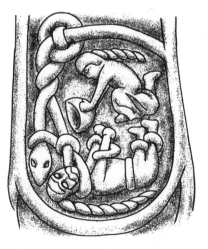

Gosforth cross depicting Loki and Sigyn

Despite the limited role she plays in the mythos, her name is still echoed and remembered throughout Scandinavia: Norwegians have named two varieties of wheat after her, and Sweden christened a (now retired) nuclear fuel ship MS *Sigyn*. This last tribute strikes me as a testament to the dark humor of the Nordic people, and I can only hope that unloading the dangerous fuel from the MS Sigyn didn't result in earthquakes around the world.

WHAT'S IN A NAME?

When archaeological and written records are sparse, examination of the language of names can help us to glean a little more insight into the gods and goddesses. After all, a lot of Norse names for deity and saga heroes tend to relate in some way or another to their appearances or feats. I enjoy the privilege of friendship with Kevin French, a heathen with a solid academic background in linguistics. He also has a penchant for spontaneous etymological rants and lectures (sometimes aided by mead and whisky, sometimes not). Kevin will likely refute this, but his brilliant mind offers a number of interesting perspectives on things we take for granted in our language.

One night, following a sumbel his kindred hosted to celebrate The Troth's 2018 repeal of the infamous Loki Ban, he spoke about the etymology of Sigyn's name while he and I were engaged in a fierce competition for the resident cat's attention. During the ritual, I had hailed Sigyn, referring to her as our Victory Woman. This kenning is one of the most common for Sigyn in modern heathenry, based on the widespread acceptance of the name being Old Norse for "Victorious Girl-friend"

I could give you a shoddy paraphrase of what he said to me, but I would do the matter injustice. Instead, he graciously provided me with a copy of his dissertation, "We Need to Talk About Gefjun: Toward a New Etymology of an Old Icelandic Theonym." He acknowledged that "the name itself is usually believed to be composed of sig- 'victory' and *vin f. (female) friend" but the latter is unattested."[8] When something is unattested, the word in question (preceded with an asterisk) doesn't actually appear in original sources. In other words, if you were to hit "Ctrl + F" in documents from the old days, your search for "vin" as a female friend would not generate any results.

Kevin says -yn is a "contracted form of -vin (giving the example Bjǫrgvin to Bjǫrgyn for Bergen, Norway), and -vin means meadow in these other examples. Meanwhile, the "[Old Norse' word for 'friend' is *vinr*, so some have proposed a feminine equivalent *vin*, but importantly, this word doesn't actually exist anywhere else, and there already *is* a feminine equivalent (*vina*)."[9] This was brewing in Kevin's mind after I hailed Sigyn as Victory Woman in sumbel that night, and I was delighted to hear his scholarship on the matter.

According to Kevin, the -yn part of Sigyn's name is more likely to be related to the word "wunjo," which is familiar to most as the name of the rune representing joy. "Wyn" is "very common in Old English compound names. It can be reconstructed to ... wunjo, which would most likely result in an Old

8. French, Kevin. 2014. "We Need to Talk About Gefjun: Toward a New Etymology of an Old Icelandic Theonym." MA Thesis, University of Iceland.

9. Kevin French, email message to author, September 19, 2020

Icelandic -yn."[10] He goes on to tell me that others in the field of etymology have rethought the "Sig" as "victory" concept as well: " ... Ásgeir Magnússon and de Vries endorsed reanalyzing it as *sig* 'rope which is let down ... ' It also refers to 'rappelling,' and is related to the verb *síga* 'to ... be lowered.'"[11] This falls a little more in line with characterizing Sigyn as a goddess as it relates to her role in the lore: "Sigyn 'descends' into the cave where Loki is bound and provides him with ... well maybe not 'joy' but at least a reprieve ... "[12]

Sigyn as "Victory Girl-Friend," or as "lowered down to provide comfort"? The latter isn't as catchy or as snappy, but it pings as more accurate. It's certainly a better representation of who she is at her core. The heroic journey Joseph Campbell wrote about in his book, *Hero With a Thousand Faces*, could well apply to Sigyn as well. After all, Professor Campbell has explored the concept of the hero's journey in the mythology and folklore around the world, and every culture offers their own version of this idea. Sigyn fulfils this role in Norse mythology: like others in tales ancient and modern, she is the one to leave the comfort of home and descend to an underworld of sorts. Trials are endured, new perspectives are gained, and the hero returns home wiser and a greater boon to their community. Alas, the Eddas don't complete the cycle in regards to Sigyn's homecoming and the insights about what it means to be a hero, but modern heathens reap the benefits of her descent into the cave. We recognize the

10. French, Kevin. 2014. "We Need to Talk About Gefjun: Toward a New Etymology of an Old Icelandic Theonym."

11. French, 2020.

12. French, 2020.

compassion and the loyalty she embodies, and we look to her for guidance in providing comfort and support to those in our own lives not because of the rewards and recognition we might gain, but because it simply must be done.

WHAT'S *REALLY* IN THE BOWL?

When reflecting on the myth about Utgard-Loki and the implications of Loki as sacred fire contrasted with Logi as wildfire, I touched on a fascinating idea suggested by author Dagulf Loptson. Scholar and linguist Riccardo Ginevra has researched the etymology within fire myths, and his conclusions align nicely with Loptson's theories.[13] Both suggest an alternate theory about the role Loki and Sigyn may have played in regards to ritual, roles that were warped and twisted with the Christianization of Scandinavia. As discussed in the previous chapter, Loptson's work examines the notion of Loki as a fire god, suggesting through copious research the possibility that Loki represents the sacred fire in which offerings are burned and that Sigyn's kenning "Incantation Fetter" refers to the corresponding role as making the fire sacred through use of runic chants and putting the offerings into the flames. When the myths were finally written down by a Christian poet-historian a few hundred years after conversion, he muses that their roles were altered into that of the bound god and his beleaguered wife. The image of a woman holding the bowl of offerings over the sacred

---

13. Ginevra, Riccardo. 2020. "How Linguistics Helps Us Reconstruct Ancient Fire Mythology." The Philological Society Blog. October 6, 2020.

flame was changed to that of a woman holding a bowl over her husband's face to protect him from the dripping venom.[14]

Ginevra echoes this concept in his argument for Sigyn's name having roots in the Proto-Indo-European (sei̯ku̯-n-i̯éh) and Proto-Germanic (*Sīgunjō*) languages. Etymological dissection of these words lends to interpreting her name as "She of the Pouring," emphasizing the lines in the Eddas about the action of pouring/draining the bowl when the venom fills it. From this he extends the act of pouring to be indicative of emptying offering bowls of liquids and libations into sacred fire.[15]

Kevin's self-described "chronic linguist brain" mulled over these theories and he reached out to offer some insight in terms that can be appreciated by those of us with "WTF even *are* linguistics?" brains. He thinks Ginevra is onto something with Sigyn as "She of the Pouring":

> Riccardo Ginevra noticed that it fits better with the metrics of Norse poetry if Sigyn's name is actually *Sígyn*, with a long "í," which has consequences for interpreting her name. He derives it not from any Old Norse word directly, but from Proto-Indo-European. According to him, Sigyn's name comes from the PIE root *sei̯ku̯- meaning 'to pour,' plus a suffix also found in the goddess names *Hlóðyn* and *Fjörgyn*, and interprets her name 'she

14. Loptson, Dagulf. 2019. *Playing With Fire: An Exploration of Loki Laufeyjarson*. Lulu Enterprises.

15. Ginevra, Riccardo. 2018. "Old Norse Sígyn (*sei̯ k U̯ -Ṇ -Į Éh 2 -'she of the Pouring'), Vedic °sécanī-'pouring', Celtic Sēquana and PIE *sei̯ k U̯ -'pour'*." Edited by David Goldstein, Stephanie Jamison, and Brent Vine. *Acadamia.Edu*.

of the pouring.' He connects Sigyn's 'pouring' and his identification of Loki as a fire god to possible Bronze Age fire rituals discussed by Anders Kaliff (2005).[16]

However, this line of thought explored by Loptson and Ginevra—that Sigyn is a goddess of pouring offerings into ritual fire- is still speculative at best. That doesn't discount the idea, and honestly, it's in line with my own perception of their role in ritual. In fact, when my kindred holds blót, we each play a role in the ritual. I tend to take the role of committing our offerings into the fire, and when I hold the bowl into which our libations have been collected, I hold it over the flames as I speak to the gods, expressing our hopes that the offerings are well-received. It's always been my favorite part of ritual, and I feel a deep connection with Sigyn and Loki both at the moment I raise that heavy bowl over the heat of the leaping flames. Is Loki a fire god/has he always been a fire god? Is Sigyn as Incantation-Fetter the goddess of singing runic blessings over offerings? Maybe. Maybe not. We don't know for sure how they were truly regarded before the Christian influence started seeping into the Eddas. The lack of concrete proof that "Loki is X and Sigyn is Y" doesn't lessen the awe I feel throughout my whole being when I stand before a fire with a bowl held aloft.

It's a shame there isn't more concrete evidence regarding Sigyn in the historical records, but that doesn't invalidate her as an important and valued member of the pantheon. Instead, we build the foundation of our understanding using the context clues provided in the sparse sources we *do* have at our

16. Kevin French, email message to author, November 20, 2020.

disposal. From the analysis of what we have available, we can develop our understanding further with the deities through our own devotion and practice. There are academic heathens and reconstructionist heathens, and there are plain ol' everyday practical heathens.

My perception of (and relationship with) the gods follows its own course, always dynamic and shifting and evolving. It's fascinating when my own experience or associations are echoed elsewhere, and when I'm presented with scholarly articles and debates that jive with my own concepts it absolutely sparks a rush of validation—it's exciting! That said, source materials are best read with a discerning eye, whether it be the lore or scholarly papers written by academics who know more about the evolution of language across all of its branches than you could ever hope to imagine. Critical thought and analysis is a vital skill, especially in terms of spirituality and devotional practice.

2
LOKI AND SIGYN
IN AMERICAN HEATHENRY

The mythological Loki is an ambiguous character at best. He is regarded by some as a scoundrel because of his antics detailed in the lore. Often interpreted as a villain, he's come to represent the Nordic equivalent of the devil himself. Others see him as a jester, the fool whose escapades are ripe for mockery even as he forces the truth about a person or situation. Regardless of whether he's liked or despised, he is time and again a crucial figure in the myths and stories. Thanks to his oath of blood brotherhood with Óðinn, he simply cannot be ignored in heathenry.

To be perfectly fair, he *hasn't* been ignored. He's the most hotly debated aspect of contemporary heathen practice in the United States. Sigyn is the one who seems to have been ignored by many in the American community, either due to the shunning of her husband or simply overlooking the quiet nature of her myth and character.

The Advent of American Ásatrú

The revived interest in Norse and Germanic paganism began in Europe in the early nineteenth century thanks to Jakob Grimm's book, *Teutonic Mythology*. He recounts the myths and folklore of Northern Europe's pre-Christian peoples which sparked a renewed interest in the culture that prevailed before the conversions. Unfortunately, this wasn't a purely academic work; a lot of Grimm's political ideologies are woven throughout the treatise, and they're not the most inclusive philosophies. The seeds of nationalism and cultural superiority sprang forth from this work and has plagued heathenry to the present day. Grimm's book was one of many to inspire Adolf Hitler and the Third Reich, and the subsequent use of runes and heathen symbols in the Nazi propoganda machine has had long-lasting ramifications for modern day adherents to the Nordic and Germanic pagan faith.[17]

The origins of Ásatrú ("Belief in the Æsir") itself are harder to pin down. We know that the name was used in Iceland for some time before it was finally "re-recognized" as an official religion there in 1973 thanks to the efforts of Sveinbjörn Beinteinsson.[18] While there's a strong possibility that Icelanders and other Northern Europeans were practicing the faith long before Ásatrú was formalized as a distinct religion, it's nearly impossible to cite. I'm sure I'm not the only one who comes from a

---

17. Kamenetsky, Christa. 1972. "Folklore as a Political Tool in Nazi Germany." *The Journal of American Folklore* 85 (337): 221. https://doi.org/10.2307/539497.

18. Staff. 2019. "11 Things to Know about the Present Day Practice of Ásatrú, the Ancient Religion of the Vikings." Icelandmag. January 22, 2019.

family of heathens, but there certainly aren't any records showing such. It's not as though the immigration officials listed my
grandfather's religion when he was processed through Ellis
Island in 1929. He was a proud pagan, though, I can promise
you that. So I can confidently say that there was someone honoring the old gods in New York from 1929 onward, but I just
don't have the paperwork to back it up. So for all intents and
purposes, heathenry has been alive and well in the world for
quite some time, but history points to 1973 as the official recognition of such.

The 1960s and 1970s saw Ásatrú spread in the United States
as part of the growing popularity of neopaganism and Wicca.
American history pinpoints 1969 as a defining year: a Danish
immigrant named Else Christensen founded the Odinist Fel-
lowship in Florida that year. However, her publications for the
group were more political than religious or spiritual. The '70s
saw the formation and fracturing of groups such as the Viking
Brotherhood, the Ásatrú Free Assembly, and later the Ásatrú
Folk Assembly. Like Christensen's writings, these early groups
were rife with charged politics in the vein of the völkish propaganda put forth by Jakob Grimm and furthered by Hitler.
Unfortunately, the Ásatrú movement in the United States was
plagued by racism and white nationalism from the start.

By the late 1980s, a greater divide between the bigots and
everyone else had settled in and battle lines were clearly drawn.
The Troth was formed in 1987 on a basis of inclusivity and
remains one of the largest and most easily recognized international organizations for heathens of all colors, orientations, and
backgrounds. It saw its own share of political upheavals over the

years, though; members and elders have been ousted as racialist ideologies made themselves known, and The Troth has been active in ensuring the resources they offer are truly inclusive.

Because Loki was a Nordic figure rather than Germanic, there was no place for him in the Romanticism movement of the nineteenth century. The völkish groups in Germany had no use for a deity who, in their own cultural history, didn't exist. This is a common thread in Ásatrú and heathenry today: this doesn't apply to all white nationalists and racists, but one of the dog whistles for identifying such people is the belief that Loki is *at best* a character from folklore rather than a deity counted among the Æsir.

Don't mistake this observation as a claim that people who are anti-Loki in their practice are racists. Correlation, as we know, does not always equal causation. It's only mentioned here to explain the lack of Loki in the early days of heathen practice in general.

WEAVING WYRD ON THE WEB

The 1990s: what amazing things developed with the advent of the internet. Chat rooms, message boards, and direct messaging systems led to an absolute explosion in the growth of paganism and heathenry. Where the numbers of pagans were slow and limited to mail correspondence in their rise from the 1960s through the '80s, the last decade of the twentieth century allowed for faster research and easier ways to connect with like-minded individuals. It also aided in the spread of misinformation and shady ideas with greater efficiency.

In ruminating over the formation and growth of the North-east Heathen Community, the regional group to which I belong, I reached out to a community elder who had been with the group since its inception. Stephanie Janicedottir, a resident of western Massachussettes and member of the family-oriented kindred of Úlfar aff Jera Þjóð, was in college in the '90s and originally interacted with pagans she met through groups and clubs on campus (relatable! Shoutout to Chip, who headed the Pagan Student Union at Washington College back in my day!). When the internet became more widespread, she was able to not only meet like-minded heathens elsewhere, she witnessed the shift from a purely reconstructionist mindset to more liberal and progressive leanings in Ásatrú.

In the early days, much of the Northeast Heathen Community, as well as other groups such as The Troth, seemed to be heavily populated with intense academics. A lot of discussions emphasized literary acumen and the social history of Old Scandinavian populations. To be perfectly honest, to this day I have very little interest in "Viking culture" or period pieces. I have nothing but respect and admiration for heathens who are disciplined enough to spend years studying history and archaeology and taking courses in Old Norse and Icelandic so they can read the lore in its original language without the bias of modern translators. I just don't have much to offer by way of that particular conversation.

I'm not alone in that regard: heathen communities as a whole were vaguely intimidating for newcomers to approach. Our communities tend to consist of lots of tight-knit spiritual families, and regional gatherings are more of a "family reunion" than the typical public convention. When those groups of kin got together, be it online or in person, the discussions (and eventual debates) skewed *heavily* toward scholastic matters. That's fantastic and fascinating, but if I, who had grown up overseas in a culturally Norwegian household, felt clueless and in *way* over my head during such talk, I can't imagine how nerve-wracking that must have been for people who poked their heads in looking for ideas on how to start honoring Norse and Germanic gods.

By the early to mid 2000s, American heathen communities were starting to ease up on the heavy academic reconstructionism and moving toward more practical, modern day applications of the lore to day-to-day life. During this shift, Stephanie acknowledges the struggle that a lot of heathens had in those days: the weight of Christian baggage. There's a firmly dichotomous mode of thought that goes with monotheism: if there's a force of good, there's a force of evil to balance it out, and many religions are based on the battle between the two. So if someone grows up with that line of thinking, it will carry over should they ever convert to a different philosophy. It's a difficult process to shed one world view completely and shift into a *whole new way* of interpreting the universe, so when people with monotheistic backgrounds moved into the pagan sphere, they couldn't quite let go of the concept of good versus evil.

That's when it clicked for me: I didn't have Christian baggage, but I *did* have *heathen* baggage when I dabbled in Christianity. I was never able to commit to a dichotomous mode of thought. When I read the Bible and attended my theology classes, I had a lot of trouble relating to the idea of a single, all powerful God. The concept of Christ's crucifixion bothered me to no end, this idea that "God so loved the world" he sacrificed His Son for the salvation of all. Heathen child that I was, I asked the priests, "Where's the personal responsibility? Why should someone else have to suffer the consequences of my actions instead of me?" It should come as no surprise that the priests at my school weren't as fond of me as a student as, say, my English and history teachers were. Baggage is baggage, and somewhere along the line we've *all* got to take stock of what we're carrying and discard the old clothes for new as we grow and our needs and styles change.

These lines of thought—the idea that if there's a force of Good there must be an opposing and equal force of Evil to balance it out, and the overly simplified concept that *someone* has to be the scapegoat for the good of humanity—are generally the baggage that carried over in the early days of conversion from Christianity to paganism and heathenry. Because I experienced it in *reverse*, I absolutely understand how hard it is to completely change your worldview when you start down a new spiritual path. It was strange to see it from the other side in the days of AOL: the dismissal of Loki as the negative Big Bad of Nordic religion was as vexing to me as my disdain for the crucifixion was for the priests.

Author Patricia Lafayllve brought up an excellent point regarding residual dichotomy when I reached out to her for her thoughts on Loki. She's been heathen since 1994 and a member of the Northeast Heathen community for twenty years, so I was glad to have her input regarding why Loki has been perceived as such a problematic figure in American heathenry. "Loki is not 'the devil' in any sense, nor is he 'evil,'" she wrote to me. "Good and evil as modern Westerners tend to understand them aren't really valid in the heathen mindset, and it is a mistake to use such labels when it comes to nearly anything, let alone deities."

Pre-Christian philosophy in Northern Europe isn't even remotely dichotomous. Óðinn is hailed as the Allfather, the king of sorts, to whom all others defer. He is the Father, as it were. Óðinn is *also* a ruthless, double-crossing ruler to whom the ends justify the means, and he will do whatever it takes to stall Ragnarok and save his own hide. Jotuns, the giants, are the enemy whom Thor happily smashes with his hammer, but his own mother was a giantess. Óðinn's parents were giants. Freyr marries a giantess, his father Njord is (briefly) married to Skaði, a giantess with a cult of worship of her own.

Pointing to Loki as clearly being a nasty, untrustworthy being simply because he's a Jotun doesn't work because so many Jotuns have been married and/or befriended by the Æsir and Vanir. The Jotuns *aren't* the representations of evil, they represent the raw, primal forces of nature, the uncontrollable aspects of the natural world, and the chaos and destruction things like wildfires and earthquakes can inflict. The Æsir *aren't* the bastions of all that is good, they represent civilization, human society and its structure and codes of behavior.

Regardless, in the early days of the Northeast Heathen Community (and many others across the country), that Christian baggage shoved Loki aside as a being of *negative* energy. Ray Johnson, a pagan of 37 years and counting, admits that bias in his own journey. The only things I knew of Loki were his nastier, evil side as portrayed in Christian versions of heathen myth, As a result, I fought against my own self to stay away from Loki," he says. After finding a kindred who encouraged in depth discussion of the lore, he began to see things from a different perspective. "I realized that Loki is flawed, but he is also not without merit. It wasn't until after I read the Flyting of Loki that I realized the worst offense you can do is ignore his presence."

To complicate matters, when these fledgling heathens in the early days of the community encountered pro-Loki types, the experiences left a bit (or a lot, depending on who you ask) to be desired. Stephanie recalls strife and unhealthy community dynamics caused by some of the Loki folk who shared ritual space with other members of the NEHC. Heathens take community building *very* seriously and are wary of those who don't seem to respect that. Because of the danger posed to the community in the Northeastern region, a difficult decision had to be made. Mike Smith is one of the original founders of the Northeast Heathen Community, and one night when the whiskey was teasing his hilariously outrageous Massachusetts accent out to the forefront of his impassioned speech, he clarified the thought process behind the controversial Nokean stance. When the NEHC was first forming, no one had a particularly anti-Loki attitude, as it were. At worst, if someone hailed the Trickster in blót or sumbel, there might be a few folks rolling their eyes and raising their horn in a "yeah, yeah, hail" manner, lacking the enthusiasm they'd show for, say, Thor.

It wasn't until around 1997, when some of the bad actors became more aggressive, that Mike and the others saw cracks in the community that threatened its collapse. They weren't happy about suggesting a "no Loki in ritual" stance. It was almost an act of desperation solely to *protect* the community of heathens. It worked: the disruptive behaviors largely vanished when those early Lokeans took their leave, and the NEHC went on to grow and flourish as the oldest, largest, and most closely-knit community of Norse and Germanic heathens in the United States. Unfortunately, when the bad actors left, so did a number of Lokeans who were vital to the community as they had been unfairly grouped in with the disruptors. Mike assured me that the stand against Loki acceptance wasn't something that was done with any sort of glee or personal vendetta. It was simply to keep members of the NEHC safe from unnervingly questionable behavior from certain individuals and to protect the group as a whole. They were dismayed to feel the loss of the Lokeans who helped to build the network of heathens, and they felt that loss keenly over the years and to this day look back on it with regret.

Like all healthy, strong communities, the NEHC is dynamic and willing to reassess matters as people find their footing and introduce new ideas. Loki and his devotees are as much a part of the Northeastern enclave of heathens these days as any other deity. It does us all well to remember that Loki is an integral part of heathenry, and his people have a lot of gifts and energy to devote toward building the community up and helping one another. Many NEHC Lokeans are just as quick to band with the rest of the group to protect it when bad behavior threatens anyone within. We are as much a part of the community as the Thorsmen, Tyrswomen, and everyone else.

It may hurt some to know that there's a history of Nokian attitudes, but in context of the strife being faced in the '90s and hearing accounts of what happened, I can appreciate the drive to keep the community from crumbling away to be no more than a curious footnote in American heathen history.

The NEHC isn't the only American group that has experienced Lokeans as posing legitimate threats to the well-being of the greater community. Ashli Autio, a heathen who writes about women's roles in pagan religions, specifically remarked on the lack of concern for the community when talking to me about why her tribe has a taboo in place against Loki: "For us, … it's the mean spiritedness of his transgressive nature against his innermost circle. He is representative of violence, committed from one family member to another, and with Frið a nigh divine mandate, his actions as portrayed in the literature run counter to the idea of Frið and family security."

Ashli isn't the only person to regard Loki this way. Others have expressed concern over the years regarding the harm he does to others in the myths and the way some Lokeans use his role in the lore as an excuse for bad behavior. Those concerns are valid, because they're rooted in how one interprets the myths themselves. I can't speak for those raised in a Christianized environment, but my heathen family never said, "Stay away from Loki, he hurts people, just look at XYZ story in the myths." Instead, I was raised to think the takeaway from those stories was to take accountability for my actions and own up to whatever missteps I may have taken (whether intentional or not).

This isn't to say that I'm right and everyone else is wrong—quite the opposite, really. Like everything else, our upbringing and early indoctrination shapes and filters the way we process information. Having grown up in a violent environment, my comfort was found in old folklore, mythology, and the likes of Edgar Allan Poe. Learning how to read using a book of unabridged Grimm's Fairy Tales has undoubtedly colored the way I interpret a lot of things. So when I regard the lore, my take on Loki is that he's the opposite of abusive—he owns up to his own behavior and does what he must to resolve matters and offer restitution to those he's wronged. He's not a patron of the damaged, he's a patron of personal accountability. He doesn't abide by people sowing discord and conflict without reason. The chaos he brings is the sort that paves the way for better things. The worlds he breaks aren't utopias, they're built on the lies and conveniences with which we've grown complacent, urging us to face the truth and fix things. He wants us to *do* better so we can *be* better. But of course, your response to the Loki myths will vary depending on your own background. It's all a matter of perception, *especially* with the things lost in translation from the original tellings and languages and cultural relevance over the centuries.

Naturally, this debate is going to continue because everyone who reads the myths is bringing their own background and personal experiences into the fray. There is no right or wrong in this conversation, no answer or resolution. The important thing is that we keep talking and listening to one another to better bridge the gaps of our own pasts and forge stronger communities in the future.

Loki is, among everything else, a patient deity. It took a few decades, but he could wait for the Americans to warm up to him and the lessons he had to offer. By the time the late 2010s rolled around, he was ready, and so was the heathen community.

ACCEPTING LOKI: BECOMING TRULY INCLUSIVE

In the early days, the very idea of meeting other heathens face-to-face nearly sparked panic attacks for me. The community in my region seemed to be largely composed of *heavily* academic members. While I may have grown up believing in the Norse gods and influenced by my Norwegian grandfather's philosophies and habits, I certainly wouldn't be able to hold my own in the kinds of conversations they were having. Grad students debated the various sagas and the implications of archaeological findings, slinging around a lot of terminology that went over my head. Old Norse words and complex names were brought up and I'd start wondering if I was even saying my own surname correctly. In these early encounters, it was uncomfortably clear that I was not even remotely a reconstruction type heathen or an academic. Couple that with my pro-Loki attitudes, I just didn't feel as though I had a place among the brilliant, fascinating heathens building kindreds and communities.

Heathenry is a way of life and a set of habits in the present day, not a relic to be adapted from history. I didn't know much at that point about medieval Scandinavian history or the way people lived, so I had *nothing* to bring to the table at these gatherings. I think the only thing I *ever* piped up about was about the pronunciation of "knut" in "valknut." I *refuse* to refer to Óðinn's interlocking triple triangle symbol with two syllables. I will *always* say "val-kuh-newt" regardless of how many academics and linguists say "valk-not." "Knut" is a family name, and I don't *dare* approach it without separating the "k" and "n" sounds for fear of the spirits of my father, great-uncle, and countless other ancestral Knuts shrieking up at me from Helheim.

Even with my familial experience, people would just nod at me and continue to say "valk-not." If they rolled their eyes at something as innocuous as the way I pronounced "valknut," they *certainly* weren't going to pay me any mind if I spoke of Loki and his influence on my family. So I'd often sit in a corner, drinking mead, wondering why everyone could spend hours discussing Egil's Saga but not allow anyone to say "Hail Loki" out loud. At least I was allowed to hail Sigyn during blót and sumbel, as bittersweet as that was. Sigyn, our Lady of Loyalty, bemoaned her husband's exclusion—I couldn't even reference him when I spoke to her over the horn at ritual lest I break frith with the Loki Ban my hosts enforced.

By 2017, respected Northeast Heathen Community elder Stephanie Janicedottir said the community was starting to understand that Loki was a worthy deity and his followers were just as keen on building and supporting the heathen community as anyone else. We owe, in no small part, some of this progress to the LGBTQ+ community. Pagans and new heathens who identified as trans or bi or otherwise queer were drawn to Loki in growing numbers. He was the shapeshifter who blurred the lines of binary gender. He was the Jotun trying to adapt to the Æsir community. He was an outcast, and his experience as the shunned and ignored made him a beacon of compassion and understanding for those rejected by their own families and their own social networks. Pagan members of the LGBTQ+

community found new homes and new families with like-minded heathens and pagans. Their adoration of Loki broke down some of the barriers in place against the Trickster, and their contributions to the growing heathen community proved his value as a deity worthy of veneration.

Ellery Thomas Leary, an archaeologist, nonbinary heathen, and cherished friend, makes deeply salient points regarding Loki's importance in the queer community:

> It's due in large part to the way he situates us in history. We're so often told that our existence is ahistorical, that queerness and transness are some kind of modern conceit or mistake. In transgressing his contemporary gender norms, Loki allows us to imagine ourselves in history, and as divine. For those of us who cannot fully identify with either the divine masculine or the divine feminine, Loki shows us a different way in an aspect one might call the divine androgyne or the divine genderqueer, and so on. And his position as eternal outsider speaks to us as marginalized people, providing us with examples of how and how not to act while reckoning with our places in society.

Furthermore, they spell out exactly why kindreds and heathens should be mindful of how they state their positions about the Liminal One. Ellery's statements are so important and so insightful that they should be read and reflected on so we can make our communities even better going forward:

Because of this, many of us look to a community's position on Loki as a way of determining whether they're safe to approach. Some may find this unfair—to be sure, there isn't a direct correlation between an individual's relationship with Loki and their attitudes toward queer and trans people—but frequently, the *way* in which some communities treat Loki reveals much about their attitudes toward anyone they might consider gender nonconforming. I'm much more comfortable with someone who recognizes and respects Loki's divinity but wouldn't personally touch him with a ten-foot pole than I am with someone who refers to Loki as "it," draws parallels between him and Satan, and so forth. The former attitude is perfectly sensible, while the latter is troubling, and is much more likely to be unsafe for me as a visibly nonbinary person.

I admit it never occurred to me that the exclusion of Loki (and how such bans are expressed) would serve as a sort of litmus for how trans and queer heathens may be treated, but I'm beyond grateful for the light Ellery has cast on the issue for me—and for all of us. It's a stunning reminder that the issues on the Loki-Noki spectrum cast long ripples, and if not handled with care, a group's ban on the Trickster can be a red flag despite the group's overall inclusivity policies. Again, it's not wrong or immoral to say, "Hey, we're not comfortable with hailing Loki here," when you're hosting an event, nor are you required to hail him during someone else's toast or event (no one will particularly notice or care if you simply keep quiet when everyone else says "Hail Loki!" in response). Not everyone is comfortable with chaos or mischief or representatives of such. We Lokians aren't trying to force everyone to worship him, we just want to feel safe and welcome in the community. This should, however, help us to look at perspectives beyond our own and ensure we're not sending anti-inclusive signals.

The language we use matters—Ellery brings up a valuable point about those who refer to Loki as "it." There are many who use they/them pronouns for Loki because our beloved shapeshifter takes on both female and male forms and roles in the lore and in their own personal experiences with Loki. As you've surely noticed by now, I use the "he/him" pronouns myself because he takes on a masc presentation when interacting with me. My experience with Loki is as a male-presenting deity, though I'll happily refer to him as "they/them" when talking with someone who uses those pronouns. I refuse to invalidate someone else's spiritual relationships or perceptions by insisting only masculine terminology be used. After all, Loki doesn't care, since he is who he is, regardless of the language used. My own dealings with Loki are with Himself as, well, him. Be they my daily devotions or heftier offerings such as this book, he has always slithered into my brain and presence as masc. What matters is respect: he, she, and they are used with respect. Referring to a deity who embodies nonbinary expression as "it" is as disparaging as referring to a member of the trans community as "it." Don't dehumanize people. Disrespecting Loki in that regard disrespects members of the LGBTQ+ community. Be aware of the messages you send with the language you use.

After studying the lore and realizing the worth of Loki's role in the mythology, Ray Johnson understood that Loki was a vital part of the growing community: "I thought I was building a community when in all actuality I was leaving out the greatest part of the actual community itself, the one that plays the self-depreciating fool. [Now when I make] offerings to the gods, I always include Loki in those offerings. In truth, my devotion is to Loki first because I have realized that I have been a fool all along." Ray might be overly harsh on himself, but he's embracing the idea that we need to take a good hard look at ourselves when we're taking on the work of building community. The value of the fool is often overlooked despite the fact that they're often the most willing to speak their truth and willing to admit fault in order to fine tune their truth into a truth benefiting their kin and network of relationships.

In the span of twenty years, American heathens had grown considerably as individuals and as a collective, refining their understanding of history and lore. The reconstructionists—those who only abided by what history and archaeology could prove—were thinning out; it was no longer imperative that there be concrete evidence of Loki worship before he could be counted among the rest of the Æsir. The "Viking culture" fascination took a bit of a back seat and the focus shifted to how to adapt these Old Ways into Modern Life. Don't get me wrong, there's still a strong reconstructionist streak, and it's awesome! But the community as a whole has developed practical twenty-first-century methodology for living heathen that doesn't require animal sacrifice (which some American kindreds insisted on into the 2000s) or celebrating ritual *exactly* as described in some Icelandic saga or another. So with the growing interest in Loki thanks to the LGBTQ+ community and pop culture influences, it stopped mattering that Loki worship has no precedent in the historical, archaeological, or cultural record in Scandinavia.

As Ashli Autio says, "[Loki] has a modern day cult that venerate him based on the positive elements of transgressive nature. Regardless of whether or not he had a huge thriving cult during the peak of the Heathen ideology, he has one now and that's to be respected. He is absolutely a god befitting the modern age and some modern practices."

Enough time and experience has passed that even the Christian burden of dichotomous thinking is falling away and heathens are looking at the ideas of the myths in a new way, a more grayscale way. Their understanding of what the myths *represent* evolved and they were no longer looking at the stories as morality guidelines á la the Gospel, but rather as complex tales representing insight into the patterns of interactions and consequences in other realms.

For example, Stephanie is a Friggaswoman. For years, the tale of Baldr's death was for her an example of why Loki isn't trustworthy, as proof of his cruelty and spite. Now, she's "realized Frigga is the victim of her own hubris. Loki as the giantess who wouldn't weep? *He's maintaining balance in the natural world!*" Besides, it's specifically *because* Loki wouldn't weep that Baldr is kept safe in Helheim during Ragnarok so that he can emerge with his brother Hod to create a new utopia.

With this evolution of understanding, new consideration was given to those who honor Loki. My kindred reversed their

"Nokian" policy so I would finally join them in an official capacity. When I sent a picture of the altar to my Mom the day I was made a member of the kindred, I included the caption, "The first time Loki is included on our altar!" She immediately texted back, "It's about time! Finally!"

And then a tiki torch caught fire, top to bottom, and we decided to incorporate a Ritual Fire Extinguisher into our regular altar setup from that point on. Subtle, Loki. Way to announce your enthusiasm about the event.

That enthusiasm is one of his hallmarks, and it's been integral in shifting perception of him as the community gains more experience. Mike Hicks of "Rune With a View" was once an open and known supporter of The Troth's Loki Ban. For twenty years, he avoided Loki partly due to "the general unwillingness of the larger faith community to invite his attention, and any attending strife. The second was several disappointing interactions with those claiming to follow him who behaved in disreputable or destructive ways…harming self or others." But as time went on and he met a wider variety of Lokeans, he began to ease up on the avoidance. Now, he happily tells me that he "perceives Loki as a genius of joyful, intuitive action. He lives a radically authentic life without excuse or apology. He is fully present, vitally alive in the here and now. More than this, he represents that which defies description. His is the ultimate mystery of quantum possibility, for what other god displays such dazzling feats of transformation without the use of spells, runes, or other tools? Loki doesn't need to rely on any outside agency. He merely chooses to alter his reality…and change occurs."

Indeed, change occurs. These, my friends, are exciting times to be a Lokean.

Stephanie and I specify 2017 as a significant year in this discussion because that's the first year the Northeast Heathen Community permitted Loki's inclusion in the véstead (area of the campground dedicated to shrines for the gods and goddesses) at our annual gathering, East Coast Thing. Erika Wren, a respected Lokean in the Northeast Heathen Community, had spent *years* contributing to the community, attending ECT, and proving herself an honorable heathen and boon to the region. She is the one who patiently, carefully eased Loki into the conversation, biding her time until enough people were comfortable with the idea of Loki that a vé for him would be permitted. And it was, in 2017.

I finally attended my first East Coast Thing in 2018. It's no small coincidence that, despite knowing of the event for nearly twenty years, I didn't actually go until there was a place for Loki there. And the following year, in 2019, I was thrilled to reintroduce Sigyn to the community. She'd been overlooked for ages because of her association with He Who Must Not Be Named, and the rare times she *was* mentioned, it was in relation to the *highly* questionable UPG of a writer of ill repute in the NEHC. So it was excruciatingly urgent (and nerve wracking) to me to approach the Vé Committee and request permission to honor Sigyn in the Véstead and hold a blót for her as part of the official event schedule. Permission was granted, and I was even asked to speak about Sigyn as part of a lecture presentation on the lesser-known gods and goddesses that year.

Erika and I snuggled Sigyn and Loki together on the same altar, their vés overlapping and blended into a single space. The energy at their shrine is extraordinary, full of joy and excitement, and I'm drawn like a moth to flame there for the majority of the nearly week-long event. It's comforting to see Sigyn finally getting some recognition and veneration in the Northeast Heathen Community, and I can only hope that this book helps to bring her back into conversation and devotional practice on a wider scale.

MARVEL MADNESS

Of course, how can I possibly write about the history of Loki in American heathenry without mentioning British actor Tom Hiddleston? His recurring role as Loki (with Australian actor Chris Hemsworth's impressively muscled portrayal as Thor) in the Marvel Cinematic Universe's films became something of a pop culture phenomenon in the 2010s and introduced a new generation of Americans to Norse mythology. Somewhere between the dawn of the internet age of growing heathen communities and the current day move toward accepting Loki alongside the rest of the gods and goddesses in veneration and worship, Marvel Studios released *Thor, The Avengers, Thor 2,* and *Thor: Ragnarok.* Ladies and gentlemen (and everyone in between), this heralded a new age of heathenry and Loki-love.

Ah, 2011, I remember it well. Before the first Thor movie hit theaters, I would be met with blank stares when people asked me about who I worshipped. As mentioned before, I've always been out and proud about my heathenry, and for years when coworkers, friends, and random people eavesdropping would ask what I meant by heathen, I'd say, "Oh, I honor the old Norse gods. You know, Óðinn, Loki, Freyja … "

"Who?"

" … you've only read the Greek and Roman myths, haven't you?"

Thanks to Thor's entrance into the MCU, everyone knows who I'm talking about when I mention my God Squad. On occasion, I have to remind people that it's not accurate to the mythology because, well, it's a comic book movie (but yes, seeing Ol' One Eye portrayed as Shakespearean Hannibal Lector is pretty on point), but it's fun to geek out with fans when they compliment my hammer pendant and know what I mean when I say it's Mjolnir.

As for Loki … even though it's based on a fictional comic book rendering, and I personally perceive the Mischief Maker as being a freckled redhead with green eyes, I've got to hand it to Tom Hiddleston: he nails the vibe. The energy is on point, the smirks, the grins, the over-the-top dramatics. And for a flashy action flick, it's served as some pretty decent propaganda for the twerp. Fans were so drawn into Hemsworth's and Hiddleston's performances that a lot of people discovered the actual mythology for the first time. And for some, it resonated and led them to an active and inclusive heathen community. As I mused in Chapter One, if Loki represented the sacred fire into which offerings were poured, when the gods were starving in the centuries after Christians took over, he went out in search of sustenance for them. If some of his methods resulted in a legion of Tumblr fandom singing his praises, well, hey, the more voices the better!

One of the unexpected perks of the Marvel movies for a long-time Loki-lover was the noticeable rise of a modern day Cult of Loki. Yes, the films are strictly fictional and only loosely inspired by the lore, but the first Thor movie did a lovely job of presenting the complexities of Loki as an outsider in Asgard. He's perpetually torn between his origins and the society which took him in, and consumed by the burning desire to just be accepted as equal, or recognized for what he can offer. Frustration mounts because he's always being overlooked and cast to the side as inherently less worthy than, say, Thor. Even though he was brought into the fold by Óðinn himself he's still regarded as the weird tag-a-long riding on Thor's coat tails (er, cape?), which mirrors the lore pretty closely. He's not inherently a bad guy, but circumstances push him past his breaking point and he starts making some pretty villainous choices, both on screen and in tales of old.

Tom Hiddleston's Loki is more obviously sympathetic than Lore Loki, and because of his stellar and emotional performance, his fans read the original myths through the filter of that perspective. This gave way to a new influx of baby heathens who didn't regard the Trickster as a pseudo-Satan. To these new seekers he was (as my Mom said a decade before) someone who just wanted to be acknowledged alongside his blood-oathed brother and companions.

Of course, a lot of the Hiddleston-Loki fan club moved on for various reasons, and when the excitement died down or they realized that heathenry is a lifestyle, not a trend, most drifted away. But we're not a religion that actively tries to recruit or pad our numbers, and this was no skin off our noses. It's just nice to see our gods and their myths become a little more mainstream, more readily identifiable … and a new appreciation granted to the complexity of one of the central figures in the lore.

Besides, as a magpie who's easily mesmerized by shiny things, I've got to admit there's a lot of pretty spiffy Loki merch to be had now thanks to Marvel.

WHERE DO WE GO FROM HERE?

The Northeast Heathen Community—and the American community at large—still isn't over the fear and mistrust of Loki. When The Troth finally lifted the Loki Ban in 2018, an unofficial decree that had been in place since 2008, it started the fight anew. Many people left The Troth, enraged at the concept of weregild being paid to Loki by holding a blót to him at Trothmoot every year for ten years, one blót for each year he was banned. A collection of poems, stories, and essays regarding Loki was even published in April 2021 as one of The Troth's devotionals.[19] Quite a dramatic turn for an organization who wouldn't allow his name to be spoken at any ritual space hosted by The Troth.

Even with the changing tides, there are people who remain wary, but aren't as militantly closed off to his influence as they once were. For instance, Kat McDermott has been a practicing heathen since 2009, and she doesn't harbor any ill will against Loki. She hesitates to associate with a god of chaos, though, because, as she says, "I don't want to *invite* chaos into my life.

---

19. *Blood Unbound: A Loki Devotional.* Edited by Bat Collazo, published by The Troth.

I have enough to deal with." This doesn't mean she's unwilling to embrace the Trickster's energy when given a unique opportunity, such as visiting a friend in Iceland who gave her "a dose of Loki. Up for anything at the drop of a hat, this friend encouraged me to step outside my comfort zone. Without him and his encouragement to be spontaneous, I would have missed out on a lot of incredible experiences … That was the kind of 'chaos' I needed."

Kat goes on to offer what's probably one of the most accurate summaries of Loki I've ever heard. "Loki is that cool, fun friend who is more than happy to take you on some potentially dangerous adventures to open up your mind a little," she muses. "You get to step outside of your comfort zone and grow in a way you maybe didn't expect to. But maybe he's not the friend you invite to a dinner party where your parents will be? Or maybe he's the kind of friend you meet somewhere, but you don't invite him over because you're worried he might steal your stuff."

As of 2020, Loki still isn't permitted to be a part of the Main Ritual at the tail end of ECT, the rite in which the offerings left for the gods and goddesses at their vés are burned in sacred fire. It will happen sooner rather than later, but until then, I'm glad for Sigyn's vé. As long as Loki is excluded from the Main Ritual, Sigyn will eschew it herself. She is welcomed at the Main Ritual, but she has made it clear to me that she would rather not leave Loki behind, so their idols and offerings stay snuggled together, side-by-side, in the darkened véstead. Loki is no longer alone that night, at least. Faithful, loving, loyal Sigyn will never leave him. How could she?

When he is welcomed into the procession for the Main Ritual, she will joyfully take her place beside him at the sacred fire. Until then, she stays with him, his comfort (and mine).

Of course, along the spectrum of people who like Loki and people who don't, there's a range of neutrality as well. Patricia Lafayllve, author of *A Practical Heathen's Guide to Asatru*, includes an essay in the end called "The Problem of Loki" in which the debate is addressed as it stood in 2013. This seems to have led many to think that Patricia is staunchly anti-Loki, but to set the record straight, she *isn't* a Nokian! In her own words:

> Despite what others have said, I am not now, nor have I ever been, anti-Loki. At the same time, I am not pro-Loki. ... We do not need to worship every deity that comes around. Not everyone relates to Freyja, or to Thor, and so on, nor do they have to. I do not worship Loki. I believe in him—he certainly exists—and whether or not he was ever worshipped in the heathen period, he is certainly revered now. But I do not blót to him, or raise a horn to him in sumbel. I remember my friend Joe Mandato once said to me, "I have a mutual non-aggression pact with Loki," and that fit my position so well that I stole the phrase. 'Mutual non-aggression pact' neatly sums up my feelings—I do not bother him, he does not bother me, and it's all neutral, really. He's a complex figure, as are all the gods, and I think it is up to each person to decide if they want him in their lives or not.

I believe that Loki needs to be approached with a great deal of care and concern for one's own well-being. I'd say that about any deity, really, but in the case of Loki—as with all trickster gods—his nature is capricious. He may be steady as a rock for some, and chaotic for others, and everywhere in between. It all depends on the situation in the moment.[20]

Wise words from a beloved member of the American heathen community, and well worth some reflection. As with all things, the matter of Loki's acceptance isn't an all or nothing deal. There's really no binary at play, more of a spectrum.

We've come a long way from the AOL message boards of 1999. I know recent converts and new Lokeans are frustrated at the general attitudes about Loki that still remain, but I assure you, the last twenty years have ushered in *extraordinary* change. Even fifteen years ago, I'd have been *flayed alive* for talking about my devotion to Loki. I was indeed caught up in a few firestorms in those early days, and I was met with a lot of cold shoulders throughout the years, and *I wasn't even introducing myself as a Lokean.* I thought I was an Oðinswoman, but that "Strong Penchant for Loki™" was enough to stir up some unease. But now...now we have a place in the community, and I for one am overjoyed at how welcome I feel at gatherings and how open I can be about my adoration for the twerp.

Hail Loki! Hail the Community!

— ✦ —

---

20. Patricia Lafayllve, message to the author, November 5, 2020.

And what of Sigyn in the American community? Well, there hasn't been too much kerfuffle about her. She's quiet in her devotion to her husband, and she's quiet in most of the community. She's the one at every gathering, every party, hugging the wall, lingering on the outskirts. This is something so many of us can relate to—I've certainly done time as a wallflower throughout the years. She watches and listens and reacts, but she doesn't step forward into the thick of it all. Perhaps she doesn't feel welcomed enough, perhaps she's just hesitant because her husband is so maligned by so many. It's certainly why *I* dawdled about meeting people in my region. However, once I overcame the hesitation, my life began anew, and I've been so much stronger and happier for it. Sigyn deserves joy, too.

She suffered just as much as Loki: they witnessed the brutal murders of their sons, and stayed in that dreadful cave together, one bound in punishment, the other bound by love and loyalty. Throughout her ordeal, she didn't—doesn't—complain. She doesn't draw attention to what she does. She hasn't *tried* to make herself as known as others of the Norse pantheon. There are fewer stories about her tapping people on the shoulder, knocking on their skulls, whispering in their ears. When she *is* discussed, there's some dissenting factions, of course, thinking she's a child bride or an abused wife. She knows her own truth, though, and she doesn't kick up a fuss when she's spoken of with derision. Speak ill of her husband or sons, and that's a different matter, but otherwise, she just goes about her business and attends to her duties without calling attention to herself.

She's quiet, but that doesn't mean she should be ignored, overlooked, forgotten. The same should be said about all of the small, simple acts of kindness and joy we encounter in our daily lives. The little bits of beauty and unity we experience are so easily overshadowed by the burning fury ignited by the bellows of awfulness. We need to remember that we can't give hatefulness power over the good we see. Misery is loud and demands forced company, but the good we do deserves our attention and gratitude. These joys and sense of compassion we experience are Sigyn's influence on the community, whether it's recognized or not. The mere fact we value such acts and employ them in our lives is enough for Sigyn. She doesn't *need* us to sing her praises, but she's been in that cave for far too long. It's time for her to come back to the community.

3
LIVING HEATHEN

O ver the years, Loki and Sigyn have found their place in the personal practice of a variety of eclectic religions and spiritualities. These deities aren't exclusive to Norse Heathenry or Norse paganism, but understanding the philosophy and modes of worship to which they are accustomed helps to build a solid foundation for relationships with them. This section is but a brief introduction to the basics of heathenry to provide context to the culture which spawned Loki and Sigyn (or the culture that Loki and Sigyn, as well as the rest of the Æsir and Vanir, spawned. The cosmic "chicken or egg" conundrum of gods and humans is an entirely different discussion altogether). Bear in mind this isn't a thorough dive into the religion, just a bit of an overview of some of the more common aspects.

Heathenry is something of an umbrella term, much the way paganism and Christianity are umbrella terms. Just as there are people who drift toward specific branches and paths within paganism (British Traditional Wiccans, Hellenists, Druids, etc.) and Christianity (Roman Catholics, Lutherans, Quakers,

Episcopalians, etc.), there's a variety of paths within heathenry, the most well known of which include:

Ásatrú: "Belief in the Æsir." Probably the most well known modern path, originating in Iceland and being officially recognized by the Icelandic government in 1973. Rooted in Icelandic and Scandinavian lore and history. Focus tends to be on the gods and goddesses in Asgard, though the Vanir are also venerated.

Vanatrú: "Belief in the Vanir." Similar to Ásatrú but with more of a focus on the Vanir tribe of deities from Vanaheim. The stronger emphasis on nature and god/desses of the natural world is the primary differentiation from Ásatrú's emphasis on community and the god/desses of society and human concerns of the Æsir.

Urglaawe: "Primal Faith." A branch of heathenry formed primarily out of the customs, folklore, and traditional healing practices of the Pennsylvania Dutch people. While Pennsylvania Dutch people have always been predominantly Christian, Urglaawe draws on traditions believed to be preserved from before conversion as well as later innovations which are compatible with a polytheistic faith that recognizes the gods found in other branches of heathenry. It also draws on sources for Scandinavian and continental Germanic heathenry, but places emphasis and priority on its own distinct cultural heritage.

Theodism: A structured, more formal offshoot of Ásatrú. Far more strict and hierarchical than most heathen paths.

Theodism revolves around the creation of formalized tribes, or theods, which are the fundamental units of social and religious life according to their view of heathenry.

Frisian Heathenry: Influenced by the practices and folklore of pre-Christian Frisians, who lived in the low country region that is currently in the Netherlands and northwestern Germany.

Anglo-Saxon Heathen: Forgive the gross oversimplification, but the Anglo-Saxons were the founders of England. Their culture was a blend of Germanic tribes and indigenous British tribes, and their pre-Christian beliefs evolved from Germanic lore.

This is by no means a comprehensive list of specific pathways within the umbrella of Northern European traditions. In addition to the modern practices based on regional history, new collectives crop up even today. Rokkatru is a controversial addendum to the family; in response to the shunning of Loki and his family in American heathenry, some who honor Loki, Angrboða, Fenrir, et al. responded by framing a subset of heathenry that focuses on the Jotuns and forces of chaos (hence the name Rokkatru, referencing faith in the bringers of Ragnarok). Rokkar are perceived as being very much at odds with the rest of the heathen spectrum because the beings venerated here (such as Surtr, the Jotun who leads the army against Óðinn and his kin) are enemies of the Æsir and Vanir. But alas, some Loki-folk felt they had little other option if they wanted to worship Loki. It became a matter of, "You don't want Loki in your sacred spaces? Then *we* don't want *you!*" and a new path was forged.

All goes to show how fluid and dynamic even a reconstructionist religion can be. Even with the wide range of flavors available on the heathen buffet, a lot of heathens don't necessarily identify with any of these. Sometimes a heathen is just a heathen. Since we don't have any all-encompassing centralized authority, we wouldn't even be able to standardize these if we wanted to.

HEATHENS AND PAGANS

Why do we use "heathen" as opposed to "pagan"? Part of it is cultural and etymological (we're overly enthusiastic about the evolution of language). The quick answer is, of course, regarding the origins of each term: "heathen" has been sourced from the various vernaculars of Northern Europe, while "pagan" is Latin.

When the Scandinavian regions experienced the coming of Christianity, the cities were the first to convert. After all, that's where the more powerful rulers and kings lived, and it was a highly political movement. The people who lived out in the heaths—the countryside and barren regions—were much slower to latch onto the new religion. Eventually, city-folk referred to the isolated heath populations "heathens" as a derogatory term. The heathens were considered ignorant hillbillies who were living in the past, unable to keep up with the modern politics and cultural shift to Christianity. My grandfather proudly used the term heathen to describe himself and his family, because by the early twentieth century it was less "bumpkin" and more "yeah, we still honor the old gods."

So that's why "heathen" and "heathenry" tend to be the preferred terminology. We also note enough differences between the general practices and theology of paganism that "heathen" is a way to separate ourselves from general pagan association (respectfully, of course). Consider it to be comparable to, say, Roman Catholicism and Lutherans. They're both forms of Christianity, very similar, but with enough divergence to necessitate a different label. There's an inherent understanding of what each group believes based on the name, and so it is with heathens and pagans.

We share a lot of concepts and practices with pagans, but the scope of our practices tend to be a bit more uniform across groups than that of pagans, for one, since heathenry is adapted or reconstructed from a singular collection of lore and historical record across northern Europe. There may be variations and spelling differences in the names of the gods (Norway compared to, say, Frisia or Normandy), but they're still pretty much referring to the same deity and the same stories.

How do the general theology and practices differ? Consider first the concept of polytheism: heathens are unanimously hard polytheists, which means we believe each deity is their own separate, unique entity or being, existing wholly independent of each other as well as separate from humans. I've met pagans who are hard polytheists, but many pagan paths are more open to soft polytheism, or the concept that each individual god is an aspect of The God deity/energy, and each named goddess is an aspect of The Goddess. Heathens generally don't follow the same calendar or Wheel of the Year that pagan groups do, and while we have a deep reverence for nature and land spirits (or landvættir), we tend to put more focus on human communities and sharing social space. Magic has its place in heathenry, but it's not as prevalent in our practices as it is among various other pagan faiths.

Heathenry encompasses all of the traditions and faiths honoring the gods of Scandinavian and Germanic lore. However, Loki isn't terribly present in Germanic tradition; combined with the fact I'm second generation Norwegian-American and was raised within that cultural framework, this section focuses on Nordic-flavored practice moreso than, say, Urglaawe.

Heathenry is categorized as a reconstructionist religion. Many heathens rely on the pre-Christian lore and archaeological record to shape their practices, and it's a slippery slope down the academic rabbit hole of historical information. There's a lot to be learned about pagan beliefs by examining the literature and burial sites, and more yet from hofs and temples that have been uncovered. Idols and pendants are among the artifacts that inspire the items modern-day heathens wear and place upon their altars.

That said, the Scandinavians of old didn't leave behind much information about the day-to-day religious practices. Many were illiterate, so the traditions passed down were oral until after the Christian conversion. Besides, the population in most of Scandinavia was scattered across homesteads in the heaths and small villages rather than centralized urban developments. Because of this, religious practices varied from region to region, town to town, hearth to hearth. There was no unified rubric or dogma that plainly detailed what the faith entailed or how it should be practiced. The same holds true for twenty-first-century heathens: we're more consistent across regions in our rituals and habits thanks to books and the internet, but there's still incredible variation in personal practice.

The agreed-upon basics are simple. In conjunction with hard polytheism, we hold that none of our gods are perfect: each one is just as wrought with complexity and contradiction as us mere humans, and their flaws and mortality are recognized and accepted. They are not distant, remote beings like the Greek gods of Olympus, but rather earthly travelers who walk among us and weave in and out of our lives whether we notice them or not.

GODS AND GODDESSES

While Loki and Sigyn are the stars of this tome, they are but two deities in a pantheon of many. As described in the Poetic and Prose Eddas, the deities largely hail from two camps: the Æsir and the Vanir. The Æsir are from Asgard and tend to be gods of society and human matters. The Vanir are from Vanaheim and are generally gods of the natural world and agricultural matters. There are also a number of Jotuns from Jotunheim counted as deities in the Northern pantheon, because even the powers that be and the pre-Christian people of Scandinavia, Germany, and surrounding regions appreciate the benefits of diversity.

The gods and goddesses you're most likely to know from the stories about Loki are:

Óðinn

Known by many names including Allfather, he is the chieftain or ruler of Asgard. A god of kings and leaders, wisdom, magic, war, and death. He sacrificed his eye for wisdom and himself for knowledge of the runes, and he hears the Seeress' prophecy in the Völuspá of the Eddas from which he learns of the fate of the gods. Despite the Seeress's words (or perhaps *because* of them) he adopts Loki as his brother by oath, and many who work with Óðinn and/or with Loki know those two are rarely too far away from the other. "Two man con" seems to be the phrase that best describes the relationship between the two.

Thor

God of Thunder, Protector of Midgard, son of Óðinn, frequent travel companion of Loki in the mythology. His favorite weapon, the short-handled hammer called Mjolnir, is a widely recognized symbol of heathen faith.

Freyja

Goddess of love, magic, beauty, sex, war, and death. Queen of the Valkyries who gets first pick of the battle slain—the left-over dead end up in Valhalla. Hails from Vanaheim but resides in Asgard after being imported as a hostage following the war between the Æsir and the Vanir in early mythic timeline. Owner of the falcon cloak that Loki often borrows. Often an unwilling bargaining chip for skeevy giants, which leads to Loki doing something to resolve the situation.

Frigg

Goddess of hearth and home, mothers, and family. Wife of Óðinn, mother of Baldr. Prone to prophetic dreams.

Baldur

The Shining One. The golden child of Óðinn and Frigg. After his death (which may or may not have involved Loki's influence, depending on which version of the myth you read), Loki refused to join all things living and inanimate in weeping for him, thus thwarting Frigg's attempts to beseech Hel to release him from her realm. As a result, he was safely sheltered among the dead during Ragnarok, and so survived the war. Emerges from Helheim after the battle's end to create a new utopia for a new generation of gods and humanity.

Skaði

Goddess associated with skiing, winter/snow, and patron of hunters and archers. She is a Jotun, daughter of the king Thjazi, and traveled to Asgard to avenge his death. Married Njord by mistake, thinks Loki's tug-of-war between his gonads and a goat's beard was funny enough to spare the lives of those responsible for her father's death.

Hel

Goddess of the dead, ruler of Helheim. Daughter of Loki and the Jotun Angrboða, noted for being half living woman, half corpse. Takes her dad's side in Ragnarok and leads an army of her dead against the warriors of Valhalla in the war.

Tyr

God of war and justice. When the Æsir used deceit to bind the fearsome Fenrir (son of Loki and Angrboða), Tyr placed his hand in the wolf's mouth as a show of trust. Once Fenrir realized the gods had no intention of releasing him, he bit down on Tyr's hand, severing it completely from his arm.

Gefjun

Goddess of prosperity and abundance. Gefjun is one of the deities invited to Aegir's hall following Baldur's death. Her presence during Loki's flyting in the Poetic Edda's *Lokasenna* is notable as she's the one to call out Loki for his bad behavior. Rather than sling barbs back at Loki, she tries to deescalate the unfolding situation by asking him *why* he's breaking the peace. When Loki turns his ire onto her in response, Óðinn himself comes to her defense. From this we learn that she is equal to the Allfather in her knowledge of the fates of the gods and humanity. Might this suggest Gefjun tried to calm Loki down because she knew the true consequences that would follow the flyting?

Heimdallr

The guard who stands watch at Bifrost, the rainbow bridge that connects the nine realms. He and Loki have a contentious relationship having once fought each other in the guise of seals. They are fated to kill one another at Ragnarok.

FRITH AND WYRD

Heathens value family and community so strongly that it's very much a defining characteristic of the faith. Oftentimes, who we call family isn't defined by blood but rather by the bonds we forge and the frith we build together. Just as our pre-Christian predecessors had hearth cults and practices unique to each household, we develop our own cults and habits with our chosen families called kindreds or tribes. Our communities are the larger collective of kindreds/tribes and solitary practitioners in a given region. In the age of technology, we have the incredible privilege of being able to build widespread communities (the one to which I belong, the Northeast Heathen Community, has members spanning from Canada to Virginia, and the expats who have emigrated to Iceland and Norway are able to stay connected with the rest of us and join in on our annual gathering!). While heathens on the East Coast may do things a little differently than the heathens on the West Coast, the ease in sharing ideas and discussing the whys and hows of regional differences helps to not only shape regional identities, but enrich our ever-evolving practices as new ideas drift from kindred to tribe to community.

No matter where we build our communities, the concepts of frith and wyrd have become the universal foundations. In eras gone by, frith (an Old English word) was defined as safety and protection, something along the lines of sanctuary. It was something of a legal concept borne of constantly warring tribes and groups.[21] Today, it encompasses the idea of creating a kind

---

21. Joseph Bosworth, T. Northcote Toller, and A. Campbell. *An Anglo-Saxon Dictionary: Based on the Manuscript Collections of Joseph Bosworth* (London: Oxford University Press, 1992).

of safe space, the understanding that when we gather, we do so in good faith. We extend hospitality and receive hospitality in turn. We forge and strengthen the bonds of friendship and equality, we look out for one another, and we act with honor and respect. We work together to ensure each of us has what is needed, to support each other mentally and emotionally as well as physically, and even challenge each other academically and spiritually to ensure we don't grow stagnant or complacent in our ways (aha! Proof that Loki has a valuable role in American heathenry, no?).

Wyrd is a more esoteric concept than frith, and they're inextricably linked. Wyrd is the cosmic web of fate and destiny that we weave ourselves and with each other. The Norns, our version of The Fates, weave our wyrd, and when we gather together and build community and honor the gods, our individual threads are being interlaced and knotted together in the rich pattern of our lives. This is why frith is so important to our communities, why our chosen families in the form of kindreds and tribes are so carefully created. Our fates, our spiritual luck and reputation, are being joined and interwoven with those of everyone else, so we must be careful about whose threads are integrated into the pattern and what shape that pattern takes. The gods themselves have their own wyrd as well, and their threads blend with ours as the loom's shuttle dances along the growing tapestry.

ANCESTORS

Ancestor veneration is one of the defining aspects of heathenry. This isn't to be confused with racial identity or genetic makeup: your ethnicity or country/culture of origin are irrelevant to heathenry despite what certain factions might have you believe. I and the rest of the Northeast Heathen Community are inclusive heathens, which means we have members and kin of a variety of ethnicities, sexualities, and gender orientation. We hold no frith with bigots of any kind, and we actively campaign against racist heathens and groups that exclude BIPOC and LGBTQ+ individuals. When we talk about our ancestors, we don't care about the origins of said ancestors—their deeds and reputation matter more than their DNA, which applies also to those of us who still live.

Ancestor worship is about remembering and honoring the dead, telling their stories and sharing their memory and the lessons they've taught, honoring their legacy to keep their spirits strong and close in our hearts and our habits. It's thanking those who have come before us for helping to make us who we are, to accomplish the things we do. It's raising a horn to those we have lost, speaking the names of our departed friends and relatives in sumbel. We call on them for protection and for advice, and we give them offerings in return just as we do the gods.

VÆTTIR

The vættir are the spirits of our homes and the land around us. They're generally referred to as elves (particularly in Iceland, where the government actually routes road and construction projects around places where elves, aka Hidden Folk, are known to congregate). Within the household or on a farmstead they're known as Nisser (singular Nisse) in Norway and Tomten (singular Tomte) in Sweden. The spirits of the land are often just called landvættir or landwights.

The function of house elves and land elves are the same: protection. They look after the house and those who dwell within, and they care for the land and the creatures that live upon it. They, too, get offerings. The traditional gift for Nisser/ Tomte is porridge with a fat slab of butter, but this is one area (of many) in which there is no hard and fast rule. After all, not every house has an elf, particularly in the United States. For instance, my house is Nisser-less, and I suspect that has less to do with my careless housekeeping and more to do with the lingering presence of the original owner. Instead of a Nisse, I have a ghost. So I acknowledge her, and I visit her grave (was it luck that led me to finding her burial place in the large cemetery close by, or was it she herself guiding me to stumble upon her marker amidst the thousands of identical gray slabs?) to leave her flowers and thank her for letting me share the house she loves so dearly.

When I'm hiking or wandering the woods, I leave offerings of tobacco for the local land spirits. It's not a traditional Nordic gift, but I don't live in a traditionally Nordic land. I live, like most Americans, on land that was once under the care and stewardship of indigenous peoples. It doesn't feel right to me to pour mead or aquavit for the land spirits here, but it's incredibly intuitive to make gifts of food and tobacco. And that's the beautiful thing about heathenry: we're not locked into One Right Way of practice. When the Vikings went a'travelling to far away lands, they left offerings as appropriate to the local deities. Our gods are not jealous gods, so they aren't miffed by us giving gifts to deities and spirits outside of our pantheon. If anything, it's a brilliant example of the concept of frith in action: by recognizing you're in someone else's territory and acting appropriately, you're upholding your end of the hospitality bargain. Rather than barging into someone else's home and demanding that things be done Your Way, you listen to your hosts and you learn their customs, and you participate when invited to do so. It's a delightful cultural, spiritual, and intellectual exchange that builds bonds of trust and kinship (frith!).

BLÓT

Blót (pronounced "bloat") is a catchall reference to formalized acts of devotion, or act of worship in which an offering or sacrifice is made to god/s or goddess/es, ancestors, or the vættir. Some heathens think it's derived from the word for "blood" as in sacrifice, but according to etymologist Guus Kronen, it's from *blōstreis*, a word used by the Goths as "worshiper."[22]

Blót is generally a bit more formal than sumbel, though it can be as simple as setting aside a bit of your meal to share with deity or ancestors. It can be something as elaborate as a structured, formal ceremony with prayers and chants, singing and music, altars and a fire in which to burn the offerings made by the gathered crowd. I myself engage in small, simple "snackrifice" offerings on a regular basis, and save the "big" sacrifices for when I engage in more formal blóts with my kindred and/or community.

The rituals presented in Chapter Six are examples of blóts that can be performed in a group or alone.

---

22. Kroonen, Guus. 2013. *Etymological Dictionary of Proto-Germanic*. Leiden: Brill.

SUMBEL

Sumbel is best summed up as ritualized drinking and toasting, or a ceremonial toast. A drinking horn is passed around and speeches are made in praise of gods, ancestors, and personal or community accomplishments. It typically consists of three rounds: gods, ancestors and heroes, and toasts and boasts. Depending on the supply of mead on hand and the tolerance of those participating, a sumbel can extend well beyond three rounds. We heathens tend to be long-winded and we have Lots to Say and Many to Hail. Sumbel can be a planned event to take place after a blót, or it can be an impromptu happening wherever and whenever heathens gather.

In the northeastern US and other regions, frith and wyrd play important roles in the act of sumbel. When mead (or your group's libation of choice) is poured into the horn and blessed, it represents our direct line of communication into the Well of Wyrd, and the words spoken over the horn of mead by those assembled are melded together and poured directly into the Well of Wyrd when the last of the horn's contents are offered as libation at the end. As such, an absolute rule of sumbel is to **never drain the horn.** The words spoken over the horn are fused into the mead itself, and if you drink the last of the contents, then you've broken the link between the horn and the Well of Wyrd.

If you notice the horn is feeling a little light and there's but a sip or two left inside, make it known so that the host can refill it before you say your piece and take your drink. There are few rules in heathenry, but this one is absolute: *do not empty the horn in sumbel.* Refill as many times as needed to ensure all the words of everyone present can be given over to the gods when the libation is made at the end of the last round.

This is also why it's poor form for someone to make an oath at sumbel, especially without warning: those words binding you to your oath *also* bind the rest of the participants to your oath, holding them accountable to seeing to it that you fulfil your end of said oath. If you fail or break your oath, then the bad luck caused by falling back on your word is *also* the bad luck of your witnesses. After all, your oath was mixed in with their own toasts, and delivered to the gods with their words of praise and thanks, and the threads of your wyrd are woven in tightly with the threads of everyone who passed that horn around.

Another reason for the requirement of frith at sumbel is even more simple: hospitality must be reciprocated to the host, and the host may have some personal rules or guidelines that ought to be respected when you're in their house. There are many who don't wish to hear Loki's name so much as hinted at in their homes, over their horns. Honor that, and hail another deity or tell a different story. When it's your turn to host a sumbel, you can hail Loki to your heart's content, and your guests will honor your right to do so, just as you honored their request to hail anyone but Himself at their homestead. It does no one any good, least of all Loki, to argue about household rules at ritual, or worse yet, blatantly break those rules put in place by the host who so graciously opened their homes and exposed their families and their wyrd to you.

OFFERINGS

It goes without saying that intent should be the driving force behind the offerings you give to the gods, ancestors, and vættir. Of course they're not physical beings requiring lavish feasts to nourish them and expensive wines and spirits to warm their bellies. Humans make these kinds of offerings because of the symbolism behind them: deity is an honored guest at ritual, and so we present to them the best cuts of meat, the best of what we have to offer. Unless you're wealthy enough to present elaborate and objectively "valuable" gifts on a regular basis, most offerings aren't going to be especially noteworthy to an outsider's eye.

There has been a bit of derision in the American heathen community regarding small, everyday objects as offerings. Years ago, when the pagan and heathen communities were starting to expand thanks in part to the dawn of the internet era, many converts were young, ranging from their teens to their mid-twenties. Of course, those are lean years financially speaking, so message boards and online forums were full of queries about the legitimacy of sharing what they had with the gods rather than procuring big, expensive things to sacrifice. This gave rise to the slang "snackrifice," mocking the idea of placing Twinkies upon an altar.

My attitude? All hail the snackrifice! Listen: my relationship with the gods and my grandfather/ancestors is something that I engage in daily. This is not a practice unique to me. Our spirituality and the connections we build with the divine are thoroughly intertwined in everything we do and say, regardless of where we are and what we're doing. And I don't blót daily, per se, but I do regularly sit down with a couple of drinks (usually coffee, sometimes whisky, sometimes both) and just take time out to commune with whoever's present. Few of us have the time, energy, or funds to toss a filet mignon on the altar every week, so coffee and donuts it is.

Energy—that's what matters. That's what sustains the gods. In my experience, my relationships with the gods improved dramatically when I stopped pressuring myself to provide "fancy" offerings and started offering time and energy on a regular, frequent basis. Consider it this way: in a relationship, would you rather be with the partner who's rarely around but gives you diamonds and Lamborghinis, or the partner who makes a much more modest living but always asks you about your day when you sit down to dinner every night? Neither option is wrong. What works for one family won't be ideal for another family. So it goes with spiritual families and relationships. Some people prefer a more detached relationship and lavish experiences when paths cross, others need daily companionship.

Don't fret about the regular offerings. There's nothing to be ashamed of if all you can manage for your regular personal blóts is a bag of pork rinds and a can of lager. As long as you're dedicating time and energy toward the gods, ancestors, vættir, etc., you're building relationships and connections. That tired old adage of "you only get out what you put in" applies here. Intent, the deliberate setting aside of time and space to acknowledge and hail the gods, sharing your brain space and communing with them, sometimes means more to them than a sword forged from gold thrown into a fire for them.

CLERGY

As heathenry doesn't have a centralized dogma and isn't an organized religion in the vein of, say, Christianity or Judaism, there isn't really a structured network of clergy. Many organizations such as the Troth and Forn Sidr have excellent programs for the study and ordination of clergy members within that group, but there isn't a standardized seminary for members of the heathen religion. These organization-specific programs are useful in regards to dealing with bureaucratic business on state and federal levels such as performing legal marriage ceremonies, prison outreach/support efforts, providing resources for community-building, and helping people looking for more information about heathenry.

There are many ongoing conversations in the community regarding what role clergy is expected to play versus lay people. Typically, people think of clergy as "anointed ones" of a sort who serve as a link between lay people and God/s. They lead religious ceremonies or rites, and they are generally on call to come to the assistance of members of their congregations, be it for counseling or shelter/sanctuary. In turn, they are supported financially by the parish. This is clearly something that, at present, can't be sustained within heathenry. After all, we're not centralized enough or uniform enough to merit full-time clergy who are paid annual salaries by the community (and how would we pay those salaries? Our communities are smaller than Christian parishes, and we don't meet weekly to pay tithes. I suppose we could really go hard on the reconstruction specific to the Viking era and pillage the local churches for their gold and silver, but that doesn't feel like a long-term plan).

Besides, some of the "jobs" of clergy are a bit redundant in pagan and heathen practice, so it may not be worth the risk of hiring full time clergy. The primary function of ordained clergy is to facilitate relationships between humans and the divine. Heathens are more like Quakers in this regard: we believe each person is able to commune with divinity directly, without intercession. Because of our innate abilities to connect with our gods and goddesses, *anyone* in the community can lead rituals, be it an elaborate blót or casual sumbel. You can't celebrate a Catholic Mass without a priest, but you can *absolutely* hold blót *without* a priest or a priestess.

In the kindreds or tribes that *do* prefer to have clergy officiate their ceremonies, the terminology used is goði/gothi (pronounced "GO-thee") for the priest and gyða/gythia ("GEE-tha") for the priestess. Individual groups may designate their own goði/a, or the role may rotate depending on whomever is leading the blót. Unlike some forms of paganism such as British Traditional Wiccans, there doesn't need to be both a goði and a gyða present for ritual. Whoever wants to step up and engage in a bit of public speaking and grandstanding may do so without having their binary counterpart present. The way we see it, some of the gods and goddesses in Norse mythology blur enough gender lines to represent duality (I mean, Loki is both a father and a mother. He doesn't so much cross gender lines as he saunters right down the line itself. Liminal beings and shapeshifters are pretty good about having all bases covered).

Other groups don't use a goði/a at all. My kindred, for example, doesn't have designated clergy of any stripe. When we hold blóts, we each have a role to play rather than having one person do all the heavy lifting. One person will tell the story behind the song/chant we do at the start of ritual to get into the right head-space, someone else will read the prayer to our patron Forseti, a different member will bless the mead, and so forth. Ultimately, we're all equal in our standing with the gods and with each other, so this shared responsibility works for our tight-knit spiritual family. This may not be as fluid a routine for other groups; some people truly benefit from having a bit more structure and having a designated goði/a, and some people just aren't at all comfortable standing and/or speaking in front of an assembled crowd, however small it may be.

Really, this is just a lot of words to say, "Clergy exists in some form or another in heathenry, but different tribes and kindreds are going to approach that role in the way that works best for them."

In the lore, and in modern practice, there are goði/a who don't serve a general spiritual purpose, but act as priest/esses of a specific deity. I, for instance, am a priestess of Sigyn. I am a Lokean within the community, and I am oathbound to Loki, but my devotion to him is more of a personal relationship rather than community relationship.

This is actually why I joke about being a Lokean nun—like nuns and monks in other faiths, that particular relationship is focused on my own individual growth and work I do for him specifically. I work with and honor many of the gods in the Norse pantheon, but the relationship I have with Loki is a bit more intense and all-encompassing. As such, you'll never hear me refer to myself as a priestess of Loki, nor should anyone call me such.

With Sigyn, my work is more of an outward act. I'm quite vocal about bringing her back into the community's consciousness, helping people to learn about her, and develop their own practices and ways to honor her. I've given presentations about her, I created and continue to keep the Sigyn vé at East Coast Thing, and I lead blóts in her honor at public events. I'm moved beyond expression when I see the numbers attending her blóts increase and when people gather at her vé to talk about her and share their experiences. One of the strange delights I cherish comes from people sending me pictures of the bowls they have found or made as they incorporate Sigyn into their home altars. Her name has rarely been mentioned in the decades I'd spent lurking at the edges of the American heathen community, so I've happily engaged in the work required to remind people why she's worth remembering. I have embraced the role as her priestess in my region's community, because facilitating a relationship between Sigyn and other heathens is something I do gladly.

THE GIFTING CYCLE

So how do we build relationships with the gods and frith with community? We engage in what we call the gifting cycle. It's more or less the foundation supporting every other aspect of the religion. The Gebo (the X-shaped rune in the Elder Futhark version of the runic alphabet) sums it up: a gift for a gift is how we develop ties between human and human, human and god, and god and god. Bonds cannot be forged and communities cannot be built without giving and receiving hospitality. The concept of the gifting cycle is echoed repeatedly throughout the Havamal and sagas. It's kind of a big deal.

The gifting cycle isn't limited to the exchange of physical goods. Yes, it's usually a tangible offering, particularly when giving to the gods, but the concept goes far beyond that. Friendship is a gift, love is a gift, reaching out to check on someone is a gift, making time to be there for and with one another is a gift. Prayers, poems, art, music, a dance: these things are all gifts we create and share with the gods and with each other. The energy and intent we devote to these things is what makes these gifts valuable.

Of course, the Havamal (the "Sayings of the High One" in the Poetic Edda: this poem is more or less a guide to living well as advised by Óðinn) does warn us not to go overboard with this. Stanza 145 says:

> 'Tis better unasked than offered overmuch;
> for ay doth a gift look for gain;
> 'tis better unasked than offered overmuch:[23]

This is a gentle reminder that we don't want to be annoying about it. Don't be an attention hog, because then everything you offer is cheapened. Are you giving these gifts to your gods and community out of a true desire to make them happy, or are you doing so to build your own reputation, to show off? Remember: intent is what matters. Give gifts to enrich a relationship, not to brag about your own riches. Also, if you give too frequently in the hopes of getting the gods' attention … well, just be careful what you wish for. Sometimes the greatest blessing is going

---

23. *Poetic Edda*, Lee Hollander translation.

about your business without some form of divinity sticking their nose into it. There's more to having a divine relationship than having tea parties with the gods: if they take notice, they're going to expect you to work. It's *really* going to cut into your sitting around time. So when it comes to gifting to the gods and community, sometimes less is better. After all, the more you give, the more the recipient feels obligation and pressure to return the favor.

GETTING TO KNOW YOU: DEVELOPING RELATIONSHIPS WITH DEITY

The gifting cycle is the foundation for building relationships and building frith. Before you worry about creating an altar or vé to a deity/ies, I suggest getting to know them a little better so that you know *how* to make a sacred space that makes everyone happy. The Nordic/Germanic gods, in my experience, are more like our kin and family than some distant king or ruler. In Ye Olde Days, hospitality wasn't shown by lavish, elaborate parties and gifts; hospitality was as simple as welcoming someone in from the cold and giving them ale and stew. According to my (very old-school heathen) grandfather, the pre-Christian Scandinavians were simple people, mostly farmers living in a harsh environment that didn't allow for a whole lot of fancy finery. Practicality was more important than luxury, and a lot of this mindset is still visible today in the stereotypical clean, minimalist decor and style of modern Scandinavians.

Practicality was reflected in their religious practices: because farmsteads were scattered and winter weather made travel difficult and dangerous, faith was often defined by individual families. Each family and each region had their own way of doing things, each homestead honoring their own selection of gods and goddesses. More often than not, the act of worship was centered around the hearth of the home. It was the busiest part of the house, so it was the natural focal point for honoring their deities.

Modern heathens more or less follow this mindset: practicality wins every time, and sincerity is more important than elaborate setups. We call our "congregations" kindreds or tribes because they are our chosen family. One kindred's practices will differ from another's, and there will be very different terms and concepts employed among different geographical regions. This means there's no one right way to do things. Hel, even the things I share here are based on my own experiences, studies, upbringing, and interactions with other heathens. There's no rubric for heathen worship, just commonalities such as passing a horn, emphasizing hospitality and community, and a penchant for mead.

Where to Start?

The Norse gods are often regarded as kin. The sagas and lore are full of stories about them wandering around Midgard and interacting with humans. They're imperfect beings, and they're not afraid to get their hands dirty. They are, literally and figuratively, pretty down to earth. This takes a lot of pressure off of the novice who wants to get to know them! In my experience, both in my own personal dealings and in observing others, these gods and goddesses aren't going to get pissy if the "wrong" kind of offering is made or the "right" words aren't used. (Case in point: I usually refer to Óðinn as "You old one-eyed bastard" when I'm pouring libations for him, and I've been a PITA to him long enough that he just rolls that eye when I think I'm being funny. Maybe don't start out with that kind of language, but don't fret about using casual conversation instead of skaldic poetry.) They seem to just enjoy and appreciate the effort on our behalf.

As you get to know them and become more comfortable in making offerings, you'll know what to do and when to do it. The more natural it becomes, the more you genuinely look forward to acts of worship. This sense of happy confidence then carries over into other aspects of your life, and you may find yourself offering your energy, acts of kindness, and random joy to the gods in your day-to-day dealings with humanity.

If you come from a background with a structured religion with defined rubrics for worship, you may feel more comfortable designing rituals for your offerings. It can be as simple as grabbing a horn of mead (or your beverage of choice. Alcohol is traditional, but *not* required), saying a prayer, taking a sip, and pouring out the rest as an offering. Or it can be more involved: set up a sacred work space with idols and tchotchkes, consecrate the space/purify yourself, and use chants and poetry to establish a mood and get yourself into the headspace you need for communing with the divine.

Get In, Heathen. We're Going Blótting.

"Blót," our primary term for worship, can be a fancy-pants ritual with garb and a massive bonfire, or it can be a quick devotional act of blessing/sharing a cup of coffee to say good morning to your household cult of house spirits and deities. It's the easiest way to start (and maintain) the gifting cycle with the gods.

If you're brand spankin' new to this pantheon, you can start blótting to the Æsir and Vanir as a whole until you start narrowing down who's angling to be in your inner circle. Alcohol is the traditional offering, but if you're underage and/or avoid the stuff, you're not required to get the gods buzzed. Just treat your blót like you're hosting a party: welcome your guests and offer your favorite beverages and foods, play your favorite music, thank everyone for coming and talk with whoever wants to talk.

As you get to know the deities better, you'll learn about preferences they might have: Freyja likes strawberries, Thor digs a hearty stout, Sigyn loves flowers and pastries, Eir appreciates herbal teas. Don't worry if the nudge you're getting contradicts what others offer: plenty of Loki folk give him strong black coffee, but I'm addicted to exactly that, so he asks me for the most ridiculous sugary sweet nonsense he can get his grubby mitts on to prevent me from drinking his coffee (the closer I am to a deity, the more of an obnoxious twerp I am. I'm oathed to Loki, so while I don't dare sample the cyser I've placed on the altar for Forseti or Idunn, I'm helping myself to some of Loki's coffee. *Mi casa es su casa*, and his coffee is my coffee).

General rule of thumb: if you're sharing a drink or food as an offering, don't give the gods something you yourself don't like (as in, "Ugh, this IPA is too hoppy. Gross. Well, don't want to waste it, so onto the altar it goes!") unless it's specifically requested. For instance, I'm not too keen about black licorice (I know, I'm an embarrassment to the Norwegian side of my family). Sometimes, however, Loki gets a hankering for some Jagermeister. If I can't tempt him with an alternate, I'll slink to the state store, get him a small bottle, then get the hell out of his way. Trust me when I say nobody needs to be around a Trickster when they're hitting the Jager.

If you don't blót on a frequent basis, you can splurge a bit on the gifts being offered since it's more of a special occasion. However, if you end up like me and make time for offerings regularly, then don't go all out. I have a very close relationship with Loki and Sigyn, and I'll sit down several times a week with a cuppa and a snack the way I do with friends after work. It's incredibly casual and informal, and barely anything is even said other than, "Heya, glad to have you guys around, just wanted to thank you for being awesome."

Cheat Sheet

- Don't stress yourself out and give yourself anxiety over starting relationships with the Norse/Germanic gods. As long as your intentions are honest and sincere, you won't piss 'em off. They're more interested in the energy you bring to the table than what you physically lay out on the table.

- Start simple: write a ritual if you feel more comfortable following something structured, or just have an informal sit down and say what's on your mind. Again, formality isn't a requirement with these guys, gals, and pals.

- Keep it going. You're not necessarily going to have a life-changing mind-shift with just one blót. Whether you do a weekly offering or a monthly offering or whatever, the important thing is to establish a pattern and remember it's a gifting *cycle*, not a once-and-done deal.

- Above all else, pay attention. Take notice of how you feel when you're engaging with the gods, and how you feel afterward. Your intuition will nudge you in the right direction as far as what to offer and to whom. The more you blót, the more you open yourself up to divine influence. You'll notice snippets of lyrics that suddenly strike you, or you'll feel a rush of euphoria for no reason at all that makes you feel connected to something bigger than yourself.

- Have fun! Spiritual devotion isn't a chore or an obligation. It's something to help enrich your life and your self-development. Treat it that way!

ALL ABOUT ALTARS

Altars are awesome, both figuratively and literally. They're the focal point during worship in a majority of religions, and it's fun to set up sacred space (especially in the age of Etsy!). Pagans and heathens often have multiple altars: one for a patron, one for ancestors, one for house spirits, a general one … you get the point. Some of us have the luxury of having enough land to build outdoor vés. Others are relegated to an Altoid tin of little mementos due to space limitations (or being in the metaphorical broom closet). I've seen some setups that are stunning in their simplicity and spaces that are akin to cathedrals in their splendor.

Then there's mine: absolute and utter chaos, full of dust, fox fur, and cat hair. It's lorded over by the plush Stay Puft Marshmallow Man—my favorite pop culture shapeshifter—I've had since I was four years old. Why yes, I'm describing Loki's altar. How could you tell?

I didn't have actual altar space until 2018, truth be told. I used to think of my entire house as a hof of sorts, so maintaining specific altars felt redundant. My home is full of treasures I've collected since childhood, and since I grew up heathen overseas, a lot of those things look like they belong on an altar of some sort anyway. Idols are scattered throughout, and a lot of the art I have features crows and ravens, goats, cats, and of course, foxes.

Once I oathed myself to Loki, though, he asked (nicely!) for his own space, which I was able to create pretty much immediately by consolidating a lot of his stuff to one spot. I've added to it over the last few years, and now it's so insane that I'm pretty sure Sigyn's idol has started rolling her eyes at the hoard of treasures. Honestly, I don't blame her for judging it.

My altar for Himself is a bit of a disaster, almost by design. Clutter is chaos, and chaos, to me, is comfort. Naturally, his altar reflects that. The spaces set up for the other members of my personal God Squad are clean and orderly. The vé shared by Loki and Sigyn is straight-up nonsense, and I love it. It's been overcrowded from day one, and I just keep piling more on.

It's not that I just let the consumables sit there forever, I just like to feed Loki and Sigyn. My mother is part Italian, and

I've inherited the obsessive genetic need to ensure guests in my house are fed and watered, as it were. As part of my oaths to Loki, I've formally opened my house to them. As a conduit for Loki's energy, he hangs around a fair bit. It's a privilege and an honor to make a place for them where they can relax and nothing is expected of them. Nothing, that is, except putting up with me throwing food at them. "Are you hungry? I have crumb cake! How about a vanilla cream donut? I have chocolate covered marshmallows, just let me know what sounds good. Please, have something. You're making me nervous if you don't have something in front of you. Here, wash that down with some Icelandic schnapps and coffee."

Of course, what works for me won't work for everyone. I've got the luxury of having over three decades' worth of collectibles and a house all to myself. For those sharing a residence with other humans or who are just starting out on their adventures with Loki, I can't emphasize this enough: There is absolutely no shame in having nothing but a few basic votive candles and a crystal or two. We're not building houses for divine powers to live in, we're giving ourselves a place to focus on our spiritual work. As someone with an absurdly large altar space, I'm telling you "big and fancy" *doesn't* mean better. I actually need to downsize because it's evolving from a place of meditation to "oh crud, is that a donut under the fox pelt? How long has that been there?!" revelation.

That said, it's hard to resist the lure of all of the gorgeous statues and altar cloths and offering bowls and STUFF we see on other altars and in shops. I admit that I enjoy browsing Etsy's shiny things as much as the next magpie. There's a lot of incredible things to acquire for your altar space, but *don't let it overwhelm*. You're always going to see altars that are "better" setups than yours, but no altar is better than the one at which you can actually focus and work.

OFFERINGS

I've got a little fox garden statue in my backyard, nestled into the mulch near the door. It's there that I deposit the consumable offerings once they've been on the indoor altar. Sometimes, late at night, I have my smoke on the back steps by the fox statue and I'll make my offerings out there. My way of giving to the gods is informal and comfortable. I've been working with them for so long and some of the relationships are strong enough that there's nothing wrong with lighting up a Camel in my PJs and pouring a bit of whisky while I sit in silence by the fox.

My offerings to my inner God Squad are frequent and given not so much in prayer or petition, but in hospitality. I share with them what I myself am consuming, because I am glad for their presence and company. Even though snackrifices are small, seemingly insignificant things, I only give what I myself enjoy; many times I've bought a bottle of wine or ale that looks promising with the intent of using it for an offering, but after taking the initial sip, I'm revolted and refuse to pour a libation. I wouldn't offer a guest a glass of wine that turns out to have a flat flavor and thin consistency, so why would I offer it to any god/dess? It's annoying to pour a whole bottle of wine down the drain, but better that than cause offense by pouring out a libation that I know is not up to snuff. The exception, of course, being if it's something they specifically enjoy and/or request.

When setting up an altar or vé, whether it's simple and discreet or a dramatic centerpiece, the important thing is that it's a space where you and the deity feel comfortable. It should be a focal point for mindfulness and reflection, a little touch of the sacred in our mundane physical world. Offerings should be made with intent and energy—the physical gift is simply a carrier for the essence of the spiritual, physical, or emotional energy you're transferring to the god/dess. Our energy is what feeds them and strengthens them, so even the most invaluable sacrifice can fall flat if it's given in a rote, dispassionate manner.

I wouldn't have such a strong relationship with my God Squad if I only made major sacrifices just a few times a year. If you want a solid, deep relationship with someone, you devote a lot of time and energy communicating with them and being present with and for them. This goes for gods as well as humans—you get what you give. It's almost as if there's a specific phrase that is continuously echoed among heathens... what is it? Ah yes, "a gift for a gift."

When I practiced as an Oðinswoman, the gifting cycle was more along the lines of the "major offerings/sacrifices at important times" theme. I'd occasionally offer libations of red wine (with a second glass poured for Loki, of course) in between the holy days, but it wasn't a regular thing because while I honored Óðinn and shaped my life in service to him, I was still just a bit wary of having that ol' one-eyed bastard taking *too* much of an interest in my daily dealings. With him, "gift for a gift" is a bit more demanding, and something I approached with caution.

When Loki asked for my oath to him, he taught me that a gift for a gift doesn't mean I have to brace myself for significant sacrifices, gut-wrenching sacrifices that feel almost as though a part of me is being ripped away. "You've hung around Óðinn too much," he chided once. "A gift for a gift can be as simple as a smile returning another smile, a spark of joy for a moment of happiness, companionship for company. Doesn't have to be scary." Don't tell him I said this, but Loki's a pretty smart cookie.

If I do need to ask for help or have a need for focused blessings, that's when the "big, valuable sacrifice" is made. But for the day to day, sitting down at the altar with a coffee and crumb cake is a reasonable offering. It's taking some time to settle my thoughts and refocus, saying "heya Lokes, how goes it today?" It's hospitality and a gift of time and energy. That's just as valuable a gift in a modern, fast-paced, urban society than a $200 bottle of whisky or wine, just as valid as a goat or blood. Don't compare yourself against what others do: the relationships you forge with the gods are between you and them, so do what you feel in your heart and soul.

FINDING YOUR TRIBE

When you're ready to do some meet 'n' greets and find a kindred with whom to honor the gods, the most important thing to bear in mind is that you're both the interviewer *and* the interviewee. Very little in heathenry (if anything at all) is one size fits all, and some groups are far more politicized than others. Don't barnacle yourself to the first group or most conveniently located group or the group with the coolest emblem on their banner (tempting though that may be). By all means, attend as many events with them as you're invited to so you can continue to get a feel for the dynamics of the kindred and the expectations placed on members.

So how do you start finding groups to meet in the first place? The internet, as with many searches, is a great place to start. I come from the old school of networking and meeting people through friends or hearing about events and groups on bulletin boards at a college campus or such. (*Hwæt!* That sound you hear is that of my bones crumbling to dust at that statement.) Organizations such as The Troth offer contact information for individuals and kindreds all across the country (and internationally), and social media is rife with group- and community-oriented pages and forums. The benefit to networking via social media is these groups are often closed, requiring a request to join that helps them to weed out bigots or troublemakers; this means you can approach with a reasonable expectation regarding their inclusivity before you even introduce yourself. From there you can get to know the people in your area and see when public gatherings are scheduled.

Because many of us take the concept of wyrd to heart, pressure is easily removed from both the host and the seeker by having what we affectionately call "pubmoots." This is a "come and go as you please" drinks and appetizers/food fest at a public venue like, well, a pub or restaurant. It's a fantastic way to meet area heathens and vet each other without the awkwardness of going to a stranger's house (or inversely, welcoming a stranger into your house). Before sharing a horn with someone in their family space and weaving your wyrd together, both sides should ensure that no one is getting their personal (and kindred) fates mucked up with people they don't know all that well.

TheTroth.org, Declaration127.com, and even meetup.com are good starting points in your search for inclusive heathen communities and individuals. Joining or contacting wider pagan groups will also be helpful for networking as heathens and pagans often come together at festivals and conventions, such as Mystic South and Paganicon.

4
LOKI AND SIGYN:
LESSONS ON THE SYLLABUS

"Sigyn's Joy" is one of Loki's kennings, just as one of hers is "Loki's Joy." I'm particularly fond of those names because of what they say about their relationship. Loki is the Trickster figure with a quick wit and wry, infectious grin, and Sigyn is the steadfast companion whose love brings comfort. They each inspire joy in each other in their own way and it's something we desperately need these days. So how do we incorporate their lessons in joy into our own lives? Just what exactly do they have to offer to we who welcome them into our lives? Do we even *want* them in our lives, this controversial Mischief Maker and forgotten Bowl Lady?

Yes. Yes, we do. The blessings they bestow are phenomenal and the things they teach us genuinely benefit all of us, whether we like them or not.

CHAOS AND CREATION

Chances are the first thing that comes to mind when the name "Loki" is uttered is chaos. Many in the American heathen community admit they shy away from him because they don't want upheaval in their lives and they're uneasy at the disruptions and drama a Trickster can inflict upon them. And to them I say: You're smarter than I! As someone who's had a very chaotic life, I'm the first to tell you it's exhausting. But I'll quickly follow that up with assurance that it's worthwhile, because Loki's chaos isn't meant to cause harm to those who respect him, it's meant to broaden our horizons and make us better members of our communities.

His *isn't* the kind of chaos that results in tangible loss or dangerous situations. And it's not always going to turn your life inside-out. But if you're tolerating toxic environments or relationships, prepare for him to say, "that's enough complacency, you deserve better!"

Yes, he invites a *lot* of madness, but it's not *destructive* chaos. More like "well shoot, this wasn't supposed to happen like that" situations that derail your plans/life path and pave the way to better options. If he's sniffing around you, just be open to changes that take your career and/or personal life in a massively different direction than you ever planned for. Roll with it, because you'll end up doing better than you could have ever imagined. He's not really one to let a sense of complacency lull you into a false sense of security. He wants us to keep growing and challenging ourselves to try new things so we never lose our sense of wonder at the world.

Chaos isn't necessarily a bad thing itself—everyone thinks it simply means destruction, but the thing is, when outdated modes of thought and complacency creep in, then growth stops. It's imperative to chip away at whatever is keeping you back from becoming better. There's a reason the adage "you can't make an omelette without breaking a few eggs" is so timeless: in order to make something new and better, you have to break down and destroy the obstacles around it. And I've noticed in my own life that whenever I become too comfortable or too complacent, the universe says "NOPE!" and decides that making an omelette isn't good enough—these broken eggs need to be scrambled, pureed, deconstructed into a masterpiece of molecular gastronomy. But it works out in the end. When chaos creeps into your life, it gives you the chance to be whoever you want, forge whatever path you desire. It can be a clean slate to start over if that's what you need.

KINDNESS AND COMPASSION

As an American living during the tumult of 2020 and early 2021, I've grown ever closer to Sigyn because now more than ever, I crave the comfort she brings and the lessons she offers.

In the midst of the escalating civil unrest and battle lines drawn between political extremists, Sigyn reminds me of the simple, reassuring joy that comes from knowing we're not abandoned: she didn't abandon Loki, and she's not abandoning humanity. She's helping us to bear the weight of the uncertainty which hangs over us, that ever present companion of the human condition. She's quietly reminding us that we're not alone, that compassion hasn't gone missing, that connection with the gods and with each other is still possible.

The voices of hate have always been loud and always demand attention. But the good that people do is quiet and unassuming. It's so easy to overlook the little bits of love and kindness when we're so distracted by the ugly side of humanity, but they're there, and they outnumber the bad whether we notice them or not. It's important to silence the hate and give attention and gratitude to those doing what's right, those doing what needs to be done without complaint. There are atrocious people in the world, but overall, we're pretty awesome and worthwhile. We just need to give our attention to the good we do, because the small acts of kindness are what's going to persevere in making life better for everyone.

Compassion and a smile, a laugh in the midst of the fury of negativity: that's what Sigyn and Loki are, and that's all they ask. It doesn't take much to help people around you. You don't have to change the world. Just change someone's mood for the better, and it will spread. None of us live in a vacuum, every little gesture and word impacts those around us. So in the midst of chaos, try to spread a little joy. It's such an easy thing to do, and it can make all the difference to the person at whom you smile.

LOYALTY AND LOVE

She's a remarkable lady, Sigyn. She embodies love and loyalty, compassion and comfort. Steadfast in her devotion, our Lady of the Staying Power is remarkably strong in both heart and will.

Several years ago, I sought a reading from a skilled psychic/tarot reader, and Sigyn made herself known throughout. It's my nature to be kind and patient (with everyone but myself, that is), but she reminded me that I should "never be afraid to bite." She was essentially asking me to take a page from her book: there's nothing wrong with being quiet and sweet, but when the situation calls for it, I can and *should* go for the jugular. A "don't mistake my kindness for weakness" kinda deal.

Sigyn is sweet, but holy hell is she *fierce*! This really shouldn't come as a surprise—who can picture Loki wanting to marry a pushover? He needs someone strong enough to temper his tomfoolery. He needs someone as clever and biting and intelligent as himself, and she certainly fits the mold. She's a lovely blend of gentle and bitey, and frankly, she's a good role model, and I adore her. She teases and jokes, but it's in a sweet, affectionate way. She's incredibly protective, and when things get to be a bit unfair and unfavorable, her back stiffens just as much as Loki's will. When adversity strikes she'll make it clear to me when It's Time to Bite, and Bite Hard. So I do. Granted, it's easy to take a stand when you've got gods backing you and urging you on, but victory is victory, nonetheless, and I doubt I'd be as capable of standing up for myself without that support. Her voice is quieter than her husband's, but it's just as strong.

"You know he's a good man," she said to me countless years ago when I was first confronted with the American fear and loathing of Loki. "If he wasn't, I would never have stayed with him. Trust me: he's worth loving." This, my first interaction with Sigyn, taught me everything I need to know about being loyal to those who have earned your love. And her lesson of "don't be afraid to bite" reminds me that love and loyalty don't mean you have to be a pushover. After all, the person who is most worthy of your love and loyalty is yourself. Trust me when I say Sigyn will make sure you remember that always.

HONESTY AND ACCOUNTABILITY

Thanks to this book, I've been thinking almost nonstop about anti-Loki heartache and how far the American heathen community has come around lately. I realize I usually blame Loki for fear on the residual indoctrination of Christianity and other monotheistic religions, because it certainly takes a lot of time and reflection and new experiences to shift one's world view. There's another factor, though, that scares people. Loki is a god of lies, but the point of his deceit is usually to force an uncomfortable truth. And *that*, my friends, can be *much* more frightening than simply thinking of him as a devil figure.

As more heathens become proficient at shedding ideologies that are at odds with pre-Christian philosophies, the Noki mindset is fading. People are still scared, though, because it's human nature to seek protection and security and prosperity. A lot of religions are based on seeking peace and stability. Loki. ... Loki isn't really the dude to call on for those things. He's known for shaking up the status quo. He's a chaos-bringer, world-breaker, a master of deceit to rile up the powers that be. That upheaval—even just the *possibility* of such—is scary and unwelcome in most people's lives, and that's absolutely understandable and relatable.

So how do I justify oathing myself so completely to such a being? Because I myself have known chaos and ruin, and while it's miserable, it's not without hope. When the turmoil kicks up, it broadens my perspective and allows me to see through the cracks at what's on the other side. Complacency is dangerous: it breeds stagnation, which stunts personal growth, intellectual growth, and spiritual growth. The development of skills—be they physical or interpersonal—levels off. Daily life becomes redundant and glossed over. This is when we either feed ourselves lies, becoming arrogant because we think we've reached the pinnacle, or become blind to the truth: we're not done growing, we're not done learning, this isn't as good as it gets.

This is when Loki scares the bejeezus out of us. Something happens to crack the foundation of the bland, rote life we've settled into. Some aspect of our identity is called into question. Something has come along to disrupt the predictable, familiar routines of our lives, and we're utterly blindsided by all of it. This is when it feels like everything we've built for ourselves falls apart, and we rage at how unfair it is. "What did I do to deserve this?!" And Loki answers, "It's not what you did. It's what you *stopped* doing. *You stopped caring.*"

I don't know if it's because of my military brat upbringing or what, but I've never had a problem breaking down my life and rebuilding it somewhere else, doing something vastly different than anything I've ever dreamed of doing before. I've scrapped things a few times and started from scratch more than once, and I have plans to do it again. I already have a few degrees, a few licenses, and I'm constantly plotting how to add to the collection. I've lived in the US longer than I lived overseas, and I'm ready to shift the balance there, too.

Usually, I'm my own agent of chaos: I know too well that (metaphorical) destruction paves the way for bigger, better things. Complacency makes me uneasy, whether it's regarding where I live, what kind of work I do, or even my hobbies. I find myself picking at seams, trying to loosen a thread so I can unravel a hole and see what's on the other side. I know there's infinite knowledge to gain and unlimited experiences to have, and I get crazy antsy when my daily life has gotten too routine. I need to be challenged, because when I'm challenged, I learn and I grow and I become better able to give back to my community and help the people who need it.

Of course, I have the privilege of not having a family whose needs require a measure of security and routine. I want to quit a secure job and go to school to become a mortician? Easy! Move to Iceland? Just have to figure out the quarantine situation for my cats! No need to worry about a spouse or child(ren) leaving their lives behind on account of my whims. So Loki's flair for shaking things up doesn't scare me the way it would folks who have other people relying on them for stability. I'm incredibly lucky: when my world falls apart, I have the luxury of waiting for the dust to settle so I can see what kind of potential lies ahead. It means I can embrace whatever Loki brings into my life without risking anyone else's well being. Not to say I *always* embrace his influence. Not gonna sugar coat things here: I'm just as quick to yell at him and react to his presence with some colorful hissy language as I am to curl up and enjoy his company over a cup of coffee and a smoke or two.

That said, his penchant for forcing truth can be more frightening than his habit of shaking us out of complacency.

When he's a constant in your life, expect egos to be checked on the regular: you need look no further than the *Lokasenna* for evidence of that. Ain't no time for holier than thou attitudes when he's creeping about, and that's one of my favorite things about him. Thing is, a lot of the times the lies we tell ourselves and to others are crafted as defensive mechanisms, to help us feel better about ourselves, to avoid conflict.

There's not necessarily anything malicious about these untruths, but they still damage us and stunt our abilities to become better versions of who and what we actually are. We'll craft personas and don masks to "fake it til we make it," for the benefit of fitting in, or just to keep the peace. It's a natural side effect of being social pack animals. It's a tool to help us survive … but it's not a tool that will help us thrive. Loki wants to see us thrive and become more self-actualized, and that means he's going to rip those masks away and force us to face our bare, naked selves as we really are. Yikes, yeah? Sounds scary, but it's not as bad as it sounds. Mostly because we're not as bad as we think we are.

As a mortician, I've cared for the bodies of people who have died in accidents and violence. It was—and is—crucial to me that I make the bodies presentable for their families, because it helped to put their minds at ease and move forward with the grieving process. Almost every single time I lead a family into the chapel to see their loved one, they enter tense and worried, terrified of what they're going to see. Once they see how intact and at peace their loved one looks, that fear vanishes, both visibly and psychically. Our imaginations always wind situations up to be worse than they actually are, which stresses us out and holds us back. The coroner tells the family that the trauma was severe, and they may not be able to view the body, which fills the family's collective mind with horrifically gruesome imagery. They're tormented by the thought of their loved one lying somewhere mangled and destroyed. A good mortician can restore the appearance of the body so that the family's gore-soaked imagination is eased with the assurance that their loved one is not feeling any pain, is at peace, there's no suffering any more.

Likewise, a good god can restore an anxious mind that has spun up into a frenzy of over-analyzing nonsense and has convinced itself that it's worthless and broken. The mind can and will create illusions to pretend to be something it's not. A good deity can pry the real self away from the heaps of distorted perception, the half-truth warning of "the trauma is too severe" and hold your hand when you look at yourself and see you're not as awful as you convinced yourself you were. And so you can begin the real work on yourself, the hard work: being true to yourself, being your real self without the masks and deceptions that stunt you.

Our imaginations make our perception of a situation (or ourselves) worse than it might actually be. We think we have to create masks and half-truths to hide how worthless we really are, to offer a reason why we can't do The Thing that we've dreamed of. "But the mortician analogy is flawed," you say. "There was trauma, and you used sutures and wax and makeup to hide the trauma!" Remember, Loki is a god of deception, and that deception is designed to force the truth. Yes, there is often trauma. But it's not as bad as we make it out to be. I've lost count how many times a family has come to me and said the coroner told them there were too many lacerations and a viewing won't be possible. So of course I brace myself when I retrieve the body from the morgue. And so many times, I take a deep breath, unzip the body bag... and see a face that's intact. The lacerations are minor, the mouth is slack, the eyes closed.

The important thing, the thing that the family worries about, is that the person is at peace. No more pain, no more suffering. To be able to see that, to see that yes, they have died, but their body and spirit aren't in pain, is a tremendous relief amidst the fear and sorrow. The hideous things the family has imagined weren't accurate, and while it doesn't lessen the blow of the loss, it means they don't have to work through the emotional trauma while being haunted by graphic thoughts of physical trauma. *The reality isn't as awful as it's been imagined to be.*

That's what Loki helps us with: he knows we've been telling ourselves that our true selves are unviewable, that we're too awful and mangled and broken to behold, and we need to stay covered up and hidden from others lest we repulse them. But he says, "Well, let's take a look," and he unzips the body bag, and he shows us we're not as awful to look upon as we thought. We're smarter than we thought, kinder than we thought, far stronger than we've ever given ourselves credit for.

I completely understand the hesitation to let the mask drop and let yourself be vulnerable. It's painful to confront defensive mechanisms, but there's no healing or growth to be done when we keep ourselves hidden. On the flip side, Loki can be scary if one's concerned that they'll be exposed as someone who's normal or even mediocre when they present an overly-inflated sense of ego to others. It's hard for me to conceive myself, because I definitely fall into the "I suck and am utterly unlovable" camp, but gods know I've encountered countless folks who are borderline narcissistic. Oftentimes I find myself wondering, "Oy, what must it be like to have so much self-importance when nothing they do backs up what they claim?" I get second hand anxiety from people like that, because holy crow is it going to be uncomfortable if and when they're forced to realize how much they're puffing themselves up or that other people see right through the mask of authority/excellence/superiority they've created for themselves. Fallout can get messy, and it might be scarier to be told you're really not as clever as you think you are than it is to hear you're actually not as awful as you think you are.

The fear goes both ways because reality isn't always something we can bear accepting. And a god who forces truth and challenges our cozy little ruts in life can be absolutely terrifying. But Loki's need to shake things up and have us face the facts isn't malicious; *he just wants us to be better than we are.*

That said, if you sense him nosing around in your life, or you feel compelled to welcome him into your inner circle, brace yourself. He's not acting with ill intent, but change and growth are rarely simple, pleasant things to experience. Prepare for things to get messy, learn to adjust to uncertainty. If my absurd life experiences are any indication, the benefits will be worth it. It's so much easier to hold your head up and see where you're going when you don't have masks weighing you down. And that's the god-honest truth.

HIJINX AND HILARITY

Life with Loki can get pretty … absurd. Weird things tend to happen, and the more bizarre, the more it reeks of the Trickster. More often than not, I find myself cackling gleefully at some disruption or another, eager to text someone the gory details because it's just too ridiculous to keep to myself. For instance, while writing this book, Loki was getting a little miffed at the repeated references I make of him being a weird mix of smarmy ex-boyfriend and petulant toddler. I hope it's evident that I love him truly and dearly, but facts are facts: he's absolutely an utter pain in the tuchus at times. The day I was *really* focusing on the more frustrating aspects of working with the Trickster, his energy grew crankier and crankier and he sent me a not-so-subtle warning: a friend showed up and surprised me with a homemade sugar scrub. She knows I'm a sucker for coffee, spicy, and pine scents, but for some reason (Loki. The reason is Loki) she gave me a jar of Mistletoe scrub.

Mistletoe. Not at all java-like, no hint of spice, and it doesn't smell like a forest. If anything, it smells clean and vaguely sinister. A curious offering, indeed.

It felt like a threat. An *hilarious* threat to which I responded by laughing hysterically for far too long, but a threat nonetheless. "Oh, right, because *you're* so perfect? You're a shining one like Baldr-boy? Here, enjoy some surprise sugar scrub. No one *ever* suspects the mistletoe … "

Loki. Darling. Everyone who's ever heard of you suspects the mistletoe. This isn't exactly helping to prove you're *not* a frustrating twerp.

This is one of the more tame and mild examples of the strange little quirks that arise where Loki is concerned. Suffice it to say that my kindred's motto is now, "Well *that's* not supposed to happen." My kindred started allowing the Hailing of Loki, and the same night we decided that a Ritual Fire Extinguisher needed to be officially incorporated into our altar setup whenever we gather. A giggly, sarcastic round of "Thaaaaanks LEA" erupts the moment something weird happens. I'd like to take a moment to clarify that our kindred's other motto, "Immolation is the sincerest form of flattery," was inspired by a blaze that happened long before I even knew any of them, back when they were still pretty Nokean in their practice. So in Loki's defense, it's not as though he's to blame for everything that goes awry. But there's been a definite, noticeable uptick in, um, *incidents*, starting with the night they reversed their Loki Ban.

Thankfully, my kindred delights in the weirdness. They wouldn't be my chosen family if they couldn't roll with the silly little mishaps. Now that Loki is making himself comfortable with my kinsmen and kinswomen, we're all reaping one of his greatest blessings: laughter. Loki's mischief is rarely ever malicious. If it is, there's a darn good reason for it. As long as you're being honest with yourself and avoid settling into stilted complacency, the Sly One isn't going to wreak havoc. Instead, he pokes and prods and makes himself known in order to inspire a smile or a giggle, an "attaboy" treat for forging ahead and doing what needs to be done.

My list of crazy, strange, and hysterical experiences is vast enough to fill a book of their own. The ability to laugh at myself and to make others laugh has always been a source of pride. My experience as a funeral director clued me in to the true value of humor. I started out shy and quiet, cautious and oozing with sympathy. As I became more comfortable interacting with bereaved families, I started to loosen up and allow a little more of my normal self to show through, which actually helped me to bond with the people I helped. Eventually, my colleagues started to tease me for the loud, frequent peals of laughter that echoed down the hallway during arrangement conferences. "What are you *doing* back there?! It sounds like you're throwing parties!" The part-timers, mortuary students, and funeral director interns who assisted on services often remarked on the way grieving families would hug me and thank me multiple times during a visitation and after services. "You made this so much easier than I thought it would be" was a common refrain that inspired me to keep on doing what I was doing.

My philosophy: no matter how devastated a person is, no matter how horrible and painful and raw their pain, if I spot even a tiny smile, I know they'll be okay. I didn't clown around with people who were numb or in the throes of raw grief, I was just honest with them. When going through the standard questions for completing the death certificates and obituary, I'd remark on some of the answers given and ask more. "Highest education level completed? Oh, they went to art school? That's so cool! What medium did they work in?" That almost always snapped the family out of their gloom and their faces illuminated as they began to tell stories and pull up pictures on their phones to show me.

From there, I could tease out some of the wildest memories and delight in their laughter as they shared quirks and silly habits of their loved one. It's such a simple thing to do, recognizing someone as a person instead of a collection of data, and trust me when I say *everyone* has stories and comments that will draw grins and giggles. *This* is where Loki's presence is amplified, in my experience. He saved the gods through Skaði's laughter, and he saves us through our own glee. No matter how dire or bleak a situation seems, if we can crack a smile and see just the slightest sliver of humor, we'll survive and come through the other side. This is doubly true if we're able to recognize our own folly and laugh at ourselves. The greatest blessing the Bringer of Gifts bestows is the gift of laughter.

5
ATTRIBUTES FOR DEVOTIONAL PRACTICE

The attributes and correspondence guides in this section aren't absolutes: a few are lore-based, but most are the result of decades of personal practice (not just my own, but from other heathens as well). When enough people have Unsubstantiated Personal Gnosis, it morphs into a Universal Personal Gnosis. For example, foxes aren't really mentioned in the myths, and there aren't too many foxes appearing in archaeological finds. More current folklore, however, incorporates foxes into the cultural fabric, such as in Norwegian Folktales by Asbjørnsen and Moe (Norway's answer to The Brothers Grimm, according to my mom when she gifted a copy to me when I was six years old). Because these foxes are characters who are just as devious and sly as the foxes in other cultural tales the world over, they've been linked to Loki by many individuals over the years.

Be it the red hair or the conniving nature that reminds people of one or the other, the beast is associated with the god so frequently that this attribute is considered common practice despite the lack of historical evidence that the pagan Scandinavians ever made the connection themselves.

What follows is a guideline to help you begin or enrich your devotions to Loki and Sigyn. The kennings will help you to craft your prayers and focus your intent, the colors and animals will help design your altar or make jewelry/garb/accessory selections, and the scents and offerings to prepare for blót or ritual. This is not by any means a definitive list, more of a starting point to help you connect with Loki and Sigyn. As you work with them more, you may find them guiding you toward (Sigyn) or begging like a petulant toddler (Loki) for certain items or offerings, and your list of kennings and nicknames will develop as you get to know them better.

Brace yourself: it won't be long until you're hefting a horn, ending a public blót with, "Hail Loki, Raider of Fridges!"

LOKI

Kennings are a common literary device found in skaldic poetry and the Eddas. They're descriptive phrases (sometimes indirectly descriptive) used in place of a noun, and modern heathens use kennings when addressing the gods in ritual and in writing. It's common practice to use a number of kennings for a god or goddess when calling to them in prayer during blót to heighten the spiritual drama of the experience. My favorite way to do so is to use three kennings before using the name of the deity I'm blótting to. For instance, when opening a ritual in Loki's honor, I'll say something like, "Bringer of Gifts, Fire Dancer, Liminal One, we call to you! Hail Loki!"

The following lists of kennings are by no means comprehensive; they include the most well known. You are also welcome to create your own kennings and nicknames for the gods based on their attributes (physical appearance, personality, etc.) and mythic roles. Using your own experiences with the gods may inspire kennings that are special to you and help to acknowledge your personal relationship with the deity you're addressing (e.g., Loki as Fox Friend and Sigyn as Bringer of Joy and Comfort).

When selecting kennings for prayer and ritual, consider the primary focus of the work you're doing (asking for help during upheaval or wanting to give thanks) and use kennings that refer to that specific aspect or quality of the deity you're invoking.

Scar Lip

This is one of the most common names by which I call Loki (second only to twerp) because of his loss to Brokkr in the myth regarding the creation of Mjolnir. The scars left from having his mouth sewn shut are prominent in my mind's eye.

Sly One

He's sneaky. He's clever. His mind is always spinning, devising new ways to disrupt the status quo or to save his hide after he's taken things a step too far. He's sly like a fox … and crazy like one, too.

Bringer of Gifts

This is courtesy of his role in attaining the treasures for the gods in the myth about Sif's hair. Not only does he gain gifts such as Mjolnir, Draupnir, and Skíðblaðnir, but if certain academic theories are correct and Loki represented sacred ritual fire in the heyday of paganism, then this also speaks of his duties in relaying the offerings from Midgard to the gods in Asgard.

Sigyn's Joy

The kenning "X's Joy" pays honor to the spouse, just as "The Burden of X's Arms" identifies someone via their husband or wife. It speaks well of his relationship with Sigyn. While Sigyn is known for providing comfort to Loki, this kenning reminds us that he brings joy to her as well (or did, anyway, before The Punishment). It's an indication that their relationship isn't one-sided, and suggests why Sigyn stays with him.

The Bound God

This one is pretty self-explanatory, especially since quite a lot of artwork depicts him and Sigyn in the cave in which he's imprisoned. He is tied to rocks beneath the serpent, and he may be metaphorically bound to his wyrd and fate as a key player in Ragnarok.

Father of Lies/Lie-Smith

Snorri Sturluson uses "Father of Lies" in the Prose Edda, so this one is well known but feels quite problematic to many of us who have worked directly with Loki. Catholic school taught me that "Father of Lies" is one of *Lucifer's* titles, something that author and Lokean Dagulf Loptson also mentions in her book, *Playing With Fire*. These kennings are reminders that the myths were filtered through a Christian lens when they were first committed to ink and parchment.

The notion of Loki as the Lie-Smith to many Americans may also be in no small part to his characterization in Neil Gaiman's novel *American Gods* (and because it was such a foreign association to me, it took me *entirely* too long to recognize Low-Key Lyesmith as, well, Loki Lie-Smith). My own obliviousness notwithstanding, these seem to be common nicknames for him in American heathenry. Yes, his tongue gets him into trouble more than once, but he is the bastion for brutal, blunt honesty. His deceits are usually designed to force us to face uncomfortable truths.

As always, your experiences could vary from mine, so it would be remiss of me to exclude this famous kenning just because it doesn't make sense to me personally.

Liminal One

Liminality is the threshold between places, between times, between identities. It's a state of transition, and it applies to intangible concepts such as a rite of initiation (during which an individual is neither an "outsider" nor a fully integrated member of the group), physical places such as the areas where dark forests give way to lush meadows, and the transition of day to night as the sky purples and raccoons begin to creep and bats flutter about. Loki is without a doubt a liminal creature: the Jotun counted among the Æsir, the shapeshifter who both fathers and births his offspring, the Trickster who challenges authority and social norms, instigating chaos to create a better way of being. He's a god—a divine being—but there's something seedy about him. His silver tongue can weave deceit, but all to force the truth. He is found in the between places, in the between times, when your concept of self is shifting and your worldview is altered. Loki will help you to see what's unseen and what's unknown—and what we don't *want* to see or to know—in these transient places. The initiation itself can be daunting, but if you're crossing the threshold with clear intent, the process is well worth it.

Shapeshifter

Loki is far from being the only one who can change his form in the Norse myths, but when someone mentions "shapeshifter," he's the first to come to mind. This could well be because he takes on the greatest variety of shapes throughout the lore. The Eddas and skaldic poems tell of him taking on the guise of mares, an old woman, falcons, flies, seals, and even a salmon. He is a god with neither magical items or weapons (Óðinn has Gungnir, Thor has Mjolnir, Loki has … okay, he has magic shoes that allow him to fly, but they're mentioned only once, in an off-handed manner, in the *Skáldskaparmál* when Brokkr is trying to catch Loki to cut off his head after winning the Gifts o' the Gods competition. Thor caught Loki easily, so that could well be why they're never mentioned again). He's not a brawler or a warrior. His method of self-defense and problem-solving tends to be wit, quick-thinking, and shapeshifting.

Himself

Loki is many things to many people: an archetypal Trickster, an instigator, a sneak, a problem solver. Some take his lies at face value while others see them for what they are: a clever twist of words to force someone to face the truth they've been hiding from. A fire god, a magic god, a god of mischief and chaos, a Jotun, Óðinn's sworn brother, Thor's friend, enemy of the gods. He's a bit of an [expletive redacted] but always good for a laugh. He's a clever genius with the attitude of a petulant child. Whatever he's doing, wherever he is, whoever's listening, he's always one thing: unapologetically Himself.

RUNES

Kenaz

Torch: illumination and warmth, lighting the way for our journey toward greater knowledge and exposing truth.

Ulcer/Fever: Something has gone wrong and disease is affecting the body (literal or metaphorical). Attention must be given to address what happened so healing and new growth can occur.

Berkano

Birch: Growth, fertility, womb. Loki is a mother, and his own mother is Leafy Isle, or tree. Berkano is directly associated with Loki in an Icelandic rune poem, linking both himself and this rune to secrecy, as though hiding safely among the lush leafy branches, a mystery to be uncovered. Or perhaps a nod to maternal protection—his mother keeping him safe.

Hagalaz

Destructive change that passes quickly, but there are benefits for this in the long run.

COLORS

- Green
- Red
- Orange
- Copper
- Gold

These associations are purely based on UPG and community practice. People honoring Loki tend to be a bit all over the place when it comes to colors, which is fitting for a shapeshifting tricksy type, no? I personally link green and copper with him because he presents to me with green eyes and auburn hair. This was *quite* a surprise to one of my kinswomen, who always thought of him as having blue eyes and black hair (which in turn made me laugh because she described my Grandpa Frank!). Erika, who contributed a ritual and thoughts on Lokabrenna (the summer festival celebrating Loki) to this book, almost threw the proverbial hands at me when I said "green and copper" because she *so strongly* sees him with red and orange—"He's always the color of fire, duh!"

That said, people do still ask about what colors to use for him when choosing candles or altar decor. The above list is a generally agreed-upon whittling down of the colors most commonly associated with Loki. Consider them a starting point; you'll know soon enough which colors he's going to use to rock *your* world.

ANIMALS

Snake
Falcon

Fly

The snake, falcon, and fly are creatures that have links to Loki in the myths, so their association with him in the animal sense of things is pretty much universally agreed upon. Of course, he's linked to other animals in the lore as well, such as the horse and the salmon, but they aren't used *as widely* to represent him on altars and artwork. Okay, fine, the fly isn't *as* popular a representation of Loki as the snake, but it's still a pretty significant one among some Lokeans.

Fox

As mentioned in the beginning of this section, foxes aren't mentioned in the lore. However, folklore the world over—including parts of Scandinavia—involves the crafty, sly, Trickster figure having associations of some sort with foxes. Coupled with the red hair and angular features, many tend to envision where Loki is concerned, and it's hard to think of any other animal that suits him so well.

Coyote

The coyote is well-known as the Trickster of many Native American tribes, so there's a bit of crossover here when working with Loki in the Americas. Personally, Coyote is his own spirit and too much a part of indigenous culture for the Loki association to feel natural in my own practice, but your mileage may vary.

Opossum

This is an uncommon animal attributed to Loki, but those of us who live in North America have a hard time separating the two. Opossums are pretty incredible, useful critters to have around, but have a bad rap with a lot of people. Plus, there's something so grotesque yet adorably absurd about them. Their defense mechanism of playing dead kind of suits a deity who isn't known for his fighting abilities.

SCENTS

- Bonfire
- Cinnamon
- Earthy scents
- Spicy scents
- Tobacco

POPULAR OFFERINGS

- Strong coffee
- Whisky
- Fireball Whiskey
- Jagermeister
- Red meat
- Chili peppers
- Spicy foods
- Donuts, cakes, cookies
- Candy. *Weird* candy. Don't be surprised if you one day find yourself hoarding gummy chicken feet for him.

Thankfully, these are just gummy candies shaped like chicken feet, not actual gelatinized animal appendages, but still. Strawberry-banana "chicken paws" are something I never thought I'd have in abundance, but here we are.

- Spiced Hot Chocolate
- Jalapeno Blackberry Lemonade for Lokabrenna (blackberries ripen in August)
- Gingerbread Houses. Loki loves children, and few things inspire greater glee in him than happy kids clamoring around candy and sweets they can play with!

SIGYN

Victory Woman

Despite etymologists debunking the idea that Sigyn translates to Victory Woman or Victory Girl-friend, this is still a common nickname used in ritual. I still use it myself, but not because she's a bringer of victory. Rather, in this context, "victory woman" sparks images of wives buying Victory Bonds and tending Victory Gardens and organizing Victory Drives for supplies for the troops during WWII. These women, left to tend the household while their husbands and sons were away at war, were strong and loyal, doing what they needed in order to keep the home fires burning. They were resourceful and stubborn and wracked with worry about their loved ones. They also stepped up to the plate and dominated the workforce and factories, doing the jobs left vacant by the men. They kept the spirit of Victory alive, and really, isn't that what a little compassion, kindness, and loyalty does for us all?

Incantation-Fetter

This is a kenning taken directly from the lore, and it's an interesting one: this suggests she is a goddess of magic. In the *Skaldskarpamál*, "fetter" is "god" or "deity." Link it with "incantation," or chants/songs used in magical workings, and we've got ourselves a goddess of galdr. Galdr is a form of Nordic magic, the singing of runic charms, and the word itself is Old Norse for "incantation." This ties in with the alternate theories discussed in the first two chapters of this book regarding Loki and Sigyn having once been the god of sacred fire and the goddess who makes the fire holy by singing runic charms. Once again, I recommend Dagulf Loptson as a valuable resource regarding these theories.

I personally love (and possibly overuse) this kenning because it gives greater agency to Sigyn—she is elevated from her burden and sorrow in the cave and recognized as a powerful goddess in her own right. This one evokes images of her standing proudly beside Loki as his equal, and it feels more apt than the typical "wretched wife" portrayals with which she's saddled.

North Star

Sigyn is the softly shining light that guides us in the dark, reminding us that we aren't alone and won't be abandoned. She was Loki's comfort in the gloom of the cave, and she is steady in her ways, meaning she's easy to find and follow.

Loki's Joy

The kenning "X's Joy" pays honor to the spouse, just as "The Burden of X's Arms" identifies someone via their husband or wife. Sigyn is a bringer of comfort and she loves her husband dearly. Even though this is a common kenning used for many figures in mythology and the sagas, this one just rings as literal truth for Sigyn. In my practice and experience, Loki adores her to no end and is incredibly proud she's his wife. She *genuinely* brings joy to his existence.

Grieving Mother

This one is quite self explanatory, but it's vitally important to discuss and keep in mind when working with Sigyn. She is the mother to two boys, Narvi and Vali, and she lost them *both* when the gods punished Loki. Whenever I picture Sigyn in the cave, I remember she's not only there for her husband, but also her sons. The entrails of one son are present there with her and Loki, so she can hold a wake for Narvi while she holds the bowl for Loki. Vali's fate isn't explained in the myth after he's described killing his brother, so I tend to think of Sigyn as holding vigil for him as well.

She of the Unconquerable Heart and
Our Lady of the Staying Power

These two are similar enough that they merit a shared reflection. Sigyn is very often overlooked in the heathen community because she's not a main focus in the lore like some of the other goddesses. Yet she remains ever vigilant in her dedication to us. Just as she stays with Loki despite the wretched conditions and utter heartbreak, she stays with humanity even when we don't remember her. Her quiet determination to inspire compassion and kindness lingers regardless. She has the strength and force of will to keep doing what she needs to do, no matter how tired her arms get, no matter how much her heart hurts, no matter how little her name is spoken. Sigyn is quiet, but she is resilient. She won't give up on her duties as she sees fit, and we are blessed by her influence. May our hearts be as strong and steady as hers!

Spark of Hope

This is something NYC heathen Erika Wren uses in her prayers to Sigyn, as you'll see in the Loki ritual she contributed for the next chapter. This is such a lovely and apt kenning, I thought it fit here as well. Sigyn, as she lights the way in the gloom, sparks the hope that we're worth loving in spite of ourselves. Just as she taught me that Loki is worth loving, she teaches us that we're deserving of love and inspiration. We're not alone, we're not forgotten: as long as Sigyn is present, hope never wavers.

RUNES

Wunjo

Joy and happiness. Interestingly, this is one of the only runes that doesn't seem to have a hint of negative association or shadow side to it. It simply exudes joy, which is exactly what Sigyn brings to the table.

Laguz

Water, lake. The liquid contained in Sigyn's bowl. There seems to be energy involving love with this rune.

Algiz

Protection, deep spiritual connection. Sigyn protects her husband, and her role as Incantation-Fetter creates a direct link between the gifts we give and the gods themselves.

COLORS

- Lavender
- Pale blue
- Soft, earthy colors

ANIMALS

Songbirds

These animals are linked to Sigyn through sheer UPG. Songbirds are an obvious association—when we first notice them after a long, cold winter, we're filled with hope that warmer weather and bountiful harvests are nigh. This music lifts our spirits and cheers us as we shed the weight of struggling through the dark and gloomy months prior.

Swans

Swans have an even stronger connection for me, personally. They're elegant and lovely, and they seem serene and quiet when they drift along a lake or river. As pretty and lovey-dovey as they appear at first glance, who among us *doesn't* know the dangers of messing with a swan? Don't disrespect them or pose any threat to their families or flock, or else you'll learn very quickly how terrifying they are in both ferocity and strength.

Remember one of the most precious lessons imparted to me from Sigyn: it's okay to be kind and compassionate, but don't be afraid to bite, and bite *hard*. Thankfully, I've never suffered a swan bite. Frankly, I don't ever want to be on the business end (or any end!) of an angry swan. A little bit of respect goes a long way, whether we're dealing with gods, swans, or each other.

SCENTS

- Lavender and vanilla
- Floral
- Apple and cinnamon
- Clean, homey scents

OFFERINGS

- Sprigs of lavender
- Fresh flowers
- Fruit pastries
- Remember Sigyn is a grieving mother, so donations of toys and goods as well as financial gifts to children's charities are very much appreciated.
- Volunteering time or resources to charities or organizations that help provide comfort and security to people in need
- Earl gray tea steeped with lavender
- Stroopwafel shortbread

6
RITUALS AND CELEBRATIONS

The rituals provided in the next two chapters are rituals that I have actually performed with community and on my own. Heathen ceremony is very straight forward, yet flexible. Consider the following examples as templates for your own practice. The basic structure of blót follows the exact format presented here, and you can easily altar these outlines to suit the specific intention (or deity) you wish to work with.

SACRED SPACE AND SETTING UP ALTARS

Blót can be held wherever you feel most comfortable. Generally speaking, most heathens don't consecrate a space or a circle for ritual, we just make sure there's enough room for everyone assembled to stand in a circle (or concentric circles) somewhere in proximity to the altar. Sometimes we gather near a fire pit so we can easily pour the libations and offerings into the fire at the end of the ritual, sometimes we're in someone's living room and we wander outside at the end to pour the libations at the roots of a tree or bush.

There is no prescribed rhyme or reason to setting up an altar for heathen ritual. Some pagan traditions have guidelines such as which cardinal direction you should face, specific colors for the candles, and a few required ritual tools. For blót, all you really need is a vessel for holding your liquid offering that can be passed around to everyone participating and a bowl in which to pour the libations. For sumbel, you just need the drinking vessel, be it a horn, a thermos, or a red Solo cup. That said, most of us do enjoy having a table set up with idols of the deities we're honoring and candles (sometimes scented candles) and trinkets that are special to us in order to have a focal point and that tangible reminder that we are inviting the gods to join us and sit in a place of honor among us.

Because the Sly One is a liminal being, I favor an altar cloth decorated with foxes, and I nestle my Loki idol in a fox pelt wrapped around to look as though the little beastie is curled up asleep. Sigyn's bowl is a necessity, as is Loki's horn, as they are items central to the ritual itself. Candles may be used, and the offerings given to Loki can be placed upon the altar as well for his blessing before they're committed to the fire. *Please,* if you use candles and fire, I cannot emphasize enough how important fire safety is, *especially* when dealing with someone as energetic as Loki. My kindred *always* ensures our Ritual Fire Extinguisher is near the altar when we prepare for blót.

Mead is a traditional libation used for blót and sumbel, but it is not required. Any beverage may be used, alcoholic or not.

Twilight seems to be the best time to begin a blót to Loki. Again, he is a liminal being, and it's easiest to connect with him at an in-between time or at an in-between place (such as an area where the forest meets the meadow, which is where foxes are often found).

A NOTE ABOUT BLESSING MEAD (OR LIBATIONS) DURING BLÓTS

When blessing the beverage of choice in ritual, it is common to call upon Bragi to do so. He is the Norse god of poetry; in the Prose Edda Bragi tells us about the creation of The Mead of Poetry, which bestows upon the drinker great inspiration and knowledge in the words spoken afterward. This mead was created at the conclusion of the war between the Æsir and the Vanir. To seal the truce, the gods spit into a vat and from it created a wise man named Kvasir. Kvasir was killed by dwarves, who made mead from blending his blood with honey. Óðinn stole this Mead of Poetry, and in blót many heathens ask for Bragi's blessing (and occasionally Kvasir's) over the libations that we may be inspired to speak well as we pass the horn (or other drinking vessel). Remember, the words spoken over the horn are conveyed to the gods through the libation as all who participate weave their wyrd together during the ceremony. May we all speak as well and as true as Bragi and Kvasir in that sacred moment.

RITUALS FOR LOKI

The focus of this ritual is to honor Loki in his aspect of Gift Bringer both from the lore and in the context of his association with the sacred fire into which we humans commit our offerings to the gods. Sigyn is also called upon in this blót in her role as one holding the bowl of gifts above the sacred flame.

Aside from a "well, that's not supposed to happen" quirk that occurs *at least* once every time my kindred Glitnir assembles, the following blót was an inspirational, intense event that left us feeling quite emotional afterward and oh so very proud of Loki and Sigyn. Do not be alarmed if something goes mildly awry—it's not going to offend the gods, and it's not going to ruin the ritual. If anything, laughter and sarcastic commentary is a hallmark of celebrations for The Mischief Maker.

Items needed

Horn (or other large drinking vessel to be passed around to everyone gathered)

Bowl large enough to hold the libations after the horn makes its rounds during the toasts

Candle

Idol or representation of Loki

Mead or other beverage for toasting and libations. Ensure you have enough on hand for everyone present to have a sip or two during the blót and still have enough left over in the horn/vessel to give as libation to the gods.

— ◆ —

The blót itself goes like so:

Invocation

SAY: Shining Ones, Holy Ones, Gods and Goddesses All! We ask you, Æsir and Vanir, to join us as we honor Loki, to share your presence and hear the words we speak of your friend, your companion, your headache and your laughter. Come and share this time with us and with Loki. Hail the Æsir! Hail the Vanir!

Group: Hail the Æsir! Hail the Vanir!

SAY: Incantation-Fetter, Victory Woman, Our Lady of the Staying Power, we call to you now! We welcome you, Sigyn, to join us as we honor your beloved husband. Let us hold the bowl for you so that you may rest. Delight with us as we cast away the venom and fill your bowl with gifts and gratitude. North Star, Mother of Narvi and Vali, You of the Unconquerable Heart, we call to you. Hail Sigyn!

Group: Hail Sigyn!

SAY: Bringer of Gifts, Scar-Lip, Most Cunning, hear us! We work this blót today for you, Trickster, and we ask that you be present and witness the joy we have in calling your name and the love and trust and pride we feel in counting you among our gods. Friend of Óðinn, Fire Dancer, Sigyn's Joy, we call to you. Hail Loki!

Group: Hail Loki!

Blessing of the Mead

SAY: Bragi, Kvasir, we ask that you bless this mead, to make it a sacred connection from our lips to the Well of Wyrd. May the words we speak be worthy of your attention and may the frith we build with one another extend beyond the realms so that our gifts may be well received.

Dedication of Offerings

SAY: Shapeshifter, Enchanter, Lord of Laughter, look upon these gifts we offer to you. Give your blessings upon them: they are yours. May you be nourished and strengthened by the love and praise we give to you, today and all days!

Toasts

SAY: As we honor Loki, we honor too the blood oath made between him and the Allfather. Óðinn declared that when a drink is offered to him, one must also be offered to Loki. We recognize the bond between you, Grimnir and our Most Cunning, and as we share these drinks with Loki, we offer one to you as well. Hail Óðinn!

Group, as the libation is poured into Sigyn's bowl: Hail Óðinn!

Pass the horn to each person gathered. Each individual may speak of Loki (and Sigyn—amazingly, everyone present at this hailed both Loki and Sigyn, even though the focus was on Himself!), either offering words of thanks and praise, acknowledging boons from Loki, telling jokes and letting him delight in the laughter offered, or simply saying, "Hail Loki!" As the rest of the group echoes the "hail," take a sip from the horn and pass it to the next person. It is important to note, as with all blót and sumbel, that **the liquid in the horn *must not* be emptied.** As it goes around the circle, everyone should be aware of the level of drink, and if there's only a sip or two left, ask the host to refill the horn before saying your piece and having a drink.

Once the horn has completed its journey around the circle, raise it above the altar.

SAY: Great words, honorable words have been spoken over this mead, and we savor the frith we have built as we weave our wyrd together and offer it to the great ones of Asgard as we have savored this mead and share it with you.

Pour the remaining contents of the horn into Sigyn's bowl.

Giving the Gifts

If you are around the fire/tree/spot where you pour your libations, you may proceed with the offerings. If not, have everyone retrieve their gifts from the altar and process to the area of offering.

SAY while holding Sigyn's bowl aloft: Loki, Sacred Flame, please accept our gifts we offer freely and with happy hearts. Sigyn, Incantation-Fetter, sing your galdr chants over these offerings as we give them to you and your beloved. Hail Loki! Hail Sigyn!

As you pour the libations around the fire, the group as a whole: From the gods to the earth to us, from us to the earth to the gods: a gift for a gift! Hail!

Each person present may then step forward and commit their offerings to the fire, thus ending the blót.

BLÓT FOR FACING HARD TRUTHS

This was written by Erika Wren, a NYC-based Loki loving heathen. She spends her days raising an awesome kid, drinking coffee, and trading the gods cookies for favors. She also enjoys tacos.

Loki is the candle flame that sheds light on things whether we want to see them or not. Look at the *Lokasenna*. For good or ill, Loki walked into Aegir's hall and started shedding light all over the place.

The following ritual was designed with the *Lokasenna* in mind. It is about speaking our own hard truths. Owning our own crap. It's about honesty in the face of our own fear and judgement, and action in the place of our inaction.

The ritual is a two-round blót wherein each round has its own theme. It is designed for a group but I see no reason why it couldn't be a solitary ritual as well.

Please note that the horn/drinking vessel will *only be passed in the second round.*

For this ritual you will need

Jokes. This is an excellent opportunity for sharing the cheesiest, most eyeroll-inducing jokes you've got in your repertoire.

A drinking vessel large enough to be passed around/shared

Something to drink—have enough that you can refill the vessel a time or two.

A table or flat surface

A bowl large enough for offerings

Set the drinking vessel and bowl on the table/flat surface in a place large enough for all the participants to gather around the setup.

— • —

When everyone is gathered, fill the drinking vessel and hold it up before the altar.

SAY: Loki,
Silver Tongue,
Clever Trickster,
You who exposes all things hidden,
We honor you in this space.

Pour libation into the bowl.

SAY: Help us to be brave
Help us expose the shadows that hold us hostage.
Help us lighten our burdens
Help us say the words that keep us bound.
Loki,
Problem creator.
Problem solver.
Loki,
Owner of your issues.
Master of your own nonsense.
We honor you in this space.

Pour libation into the bowl.

SAY: Help us address our issues

Help us break old habits

Help us put things to rights.

Help us be brave.

Sigyn,

Steadfast,

Gentle strength,

Protector.

Spark of Hope.

Pour libation into the bowl.

SAY: Help us find relief.

Help us find strength.

Help us find a new way.

Face everyone gathered.

SAY: The Lore is full of stories of Loki fixing problems of his own making.

He is the villain and hero of his story.

Anyone who wants to speak is welcome to come forward.

But know this:

If you step up to this altar you are speaking your truth into all the realms.

Loki was called here but all the gods will hear you.

And when you pour your truth out into this offering bowl

The burden will be shared by Sigyn.

If you step up to this altar to accept their help with your situation

You are agreeing to put in the work to fix it.

You are accepting the burden of growth.

If you are ready to take on that obligation step forward and speak your hard truth.

Step back and let folks step forward to speak.

There is a chance that people might not step forward. If that happens you can step up and say your own hard truth or you can pour out a libation into the bowl and thank Loki and Sigyn for listening to the unspoken burdens that people aren't ready to share yet.

When people stop coming forward—and I do encourage you to make a "last call" for folks to step up—top up the drinking vessel, lift it into the air.

SAY: We know from the Lore that laughter is good medicine.
Laughter lightens our hearts and eases our burdens.
Laughter, like a ringing bell, clears the air.
Loki,
You once stood before a goat and earned Skadi's laughter.
We stand now, before a metaphorical goat.
The laughter we hope to earn is our own.
The burden we hope to lighten is our own.

Pour libation into the bowl.

SAY: Help us find that spark of humor.
Help us ease the tension in our hearts.
Help us help one another.
Help us clear the air.

— ◆ —

At this point, tell a joke. After delivering the punchline, take a sip from the drinking vessel and SAY "Hail Loki!"

Depending on how many folks are attending this ritual you might want to encourage people to keep the jokes short. Please just be mindful of your ritual space and audience and remind everyone that offensive jokes aren't allowed. You will be speaking over a horn that echoes through all the realms after all. Being a good host means protecting all of your guests. The gods, in that space, are absolutely your guests.

Pass the horn. Each person tells a joke, then raises the horn and says, "Hail Loki!" and takes a sip. When the horn has made its way around, finish the ritual like so:

— ◆ —

SAY: Loki, Lord of Laughter, we thank you for the gift of humor and appreciation of the absurd to help us as we face our own worst truths. We hope that you have delighted in our shared mirth, that you have been strengthened by our laughter as we draw strength from your inspiration. Hail Loki!

Everyone gathered echoes, "Hail Loki!" as you pour the remaining contents of the horn into the bowl.

Carry the bowl to the place where your offerings are committed, whether it's a fire pit or a tree or a little patch of earth. As the libation is poured out, everyone gathered says: From the gods to the earth to us, from us to the earth to the gods: A gift for a gift! Hail!"

SOLO RITUAL TO LOKI

Loki may fancy himself a stylish, suave deity, but the truth is that he's generally very informal. In my own practice, stiff rote prayer seems (to me) like a way to detach from the gods rather than draw them closer. But again, that could be because Loki would give me a lot of grief if I tried to be so proper. Formal and scripted rites have their place, of course, especially when you're in the early stages of venerating a particular deity. Some people do better with a format to follow without having to worry about if they're doing it "right."

My regular devotions to Loki are solo acts, and they're really very simple. Most of the time, I simply set an offering (be it sweet treat, alcohol, or both) on the altar, get his attention by rattling off a few kennings, and thank him for his presence and influence. I tell him I hope he enjoys whatever I'm giving him and that it will strengthen him and revitalize him.

Other times, I get cozy somewhere with a cup of coffee and I just sit with him and Sigyn, if I sense them. I don't say any prayers, I don't use any kennings, I simply revel in the energy around me and visualize my energy supplementing theirs, "feeding" them more directly. Not that I'm a glorious power source the gods rely on, far from it! I'm just grateful for the way they both inspire me and help me along. In the spirit of "a gift for a gift," I try to share energy and spirit with them as they've done so many times before.

If you're just getting started with doing solo devotions and rituals, you can set up an altar space with the imagery, scents, and offerings listed in the "Kennings and Attributes" section of the previous chapter. Use some of the invocations and prayers from the "group" rituals laid out here, tweaking the "us" and "we" to "I" and "me."

Write your own prayers and use your own kennings, and be as formal or as casual as you feel comfortable with. Loki isn't a haughty god, nor is he easily offended. With time, you'll grow more familiar with the act of setting aside three or five or fifteen minutes a day or a week to sit near an altar or a place that feels sacred and connected to you. Bring a donut and a latte, or gummies and an energy drink, and just quiet your mind and enjoy the energy around you. Sooner or later, you'll end up snickering at something, then giggling, then falling back laughing hysterically at some wry thought or swell of euphoria.

Embrace it: that's the *real* magic of Loki.

LOKABRENNA RITUAL

This was written by Erika Wren, the taco-loving NYC Lokean who wrote the Blót for Facing Hard Truths.

Loki is a force for change. He is the fire that burns away stagnation so that we can grow.

Before we go any further, I want to state for the record that there is no evidence of a historical Loki cult. There is also zero concrete evidence that he had feast days. There are places in the depths of the internet that claim otherwise, but at this moment in time, there is no historical proof that Viking age peoples widely worshiped Loki.

Which, given the ever-growing state of the modern cult of Loki, doesn't matter in the long run. Some people like to scoff at modern Loki folk and say that we are only honoring Loki because of the Marvel movie franchise and the once-popular blogging site Tumblr.

To them, I say this: Romantic era scholars and writers were the original modern Lokeans and Nokeans. The rest of us are out here sifting through their nonsense to figure out what is real and what is based in questionable (at best) scholarship.

Whatever the reason, Loki saw a massive upswing in popularity in the late spring and early summer of 2012. When those new Loki folk asked for examples of historical and current modes of Loki worship, the internet responded with things like April Fool's Day blóts, Saturday being Loki's sacred day, and Lokabrenna.

I feel very firmly that April Fool's Day blóts for Loki are disrespectful and insulting. Loki isn't a fool, and neither are his folk. To treat us as such is dismissive, mean, and unacceptable in a hearth culture that emphasizes hospitality. Giving us "fools days" and calling us clowns isn't love or acceptance. It's mockery.

While not disrespectful, I don't think Saturdays were historically Loki's day. The first mention I have been able to find of it came from H. A. Guerber in her book *Myths of The Norsemen*. In 1909, she wrote:

> When the gods were reduced to the rank of demons by the introduction of Christianity, Loki was confounded with Saturn, who had also been shorn of his divine attributes, and both were considered the prototypes of Satan. The last day of the week, which was held sacred to Loki, was known in the Norse as Laugardag, or wash-day, but

in English it was changed to Saturday, and was said to owe its name not to Saturn but to Sataere, the thief in ambush, and the Teutonic god of agriculture, who is supposed to be merely another personification of Loki.[24]

Guerber does not provide a source for her theory, and as such, it is hard for me to take her seriously. If you want to honor Loki on Saturdays and he is cool with it, then please, by all means, do so. Just know that it is a modern practice and that there is nothing wrong with that.

That brings us to Lokabrenna.

According to Richard Cleasby—per his Icelandic-English Dictionary (first published in 1874)—Lokabrenna is the star Sirius's Icelandic name. Translated to mean "Loki's brand" or "Loki's torch," the term was likened to the "dog days" of summer by Axel Olrik.

The notion of Sirius as standing in special relation to the hot summertime ("dog days" to "dog star", cf. gr. Seirios, heat), is rather reminiscent of southern culture. The mythical origin of the name is not certain; perhaps it simply means "he who burns like fire," or the like.[25]

While certainly not the first—or last—to suggest that Loki's name means 'fire,' Olrik's comments regarding Sirius, the dog days of summer, and Loki all worked together to help

---

24. Guerber, H. A. 1909. "Myths of the Norsemen: From the Eddas and Sagas."
25. Olrik, Axel. 1908. "Loki in Recent Folklore." Heimskringla.No. Danske Studier.

create the foundation for the event that is known as both July for Loki and Lokabrenna.

Celebrating Lokabrenna

July for Loki was started by prominent Loki-friendly bloggers in 2012. They encouraged people to write blog posts every day for the entire month of July as a way to honor Loki during Sirius's (or Lokabrenna's) rising. The original plan was to post every day during the heliacal rising of Sirius—the period when Sirius rises just before or at the same time as the sun in the morning. Unfortunately, this period differs from year to year, and the dates often vary depending on location. As such, the collective of Loki folk opted to dedicate the month of July to Loki.

It has grown from a month of blogging to a month of creation in Loki's name. Art, poetry, music, and recipes all created for or because of Loki during the month of July.

Given the collective modern UPG that Loki is a god of fire—that comes to us from folks like Jakob Grimm and Richard Wagner, to name a few—it makes sense that the spark of creation is at the center of July for Loki.

If you'd like to participate in the thoroughly modern Lokabrenna movement, do a quick internet search to see when Sirius will have its heliacal rising in your area. The Farmer's Almanac states that it is from July 3–August 11 every year, but the dates do change, so please feel free to check your local times.

You can also combine the two. I make a point to talk about Loki on social media and my blog during July and add in daily prayer to him during the heliacal rising of Sirius. Below is a prayer that you are welcome to use. You are also free to write your own or to speak off the cuff/from the heart.

Freedom of expression is one of the perks of having no historical records. We get to be the storytellers and dreamers of dreams.

Prayer for Lokabrenna

Loki:

Son of Laufey

Burden of Sigyn's arms.

Your name falls from my lips for all to hear,

As your star rises in the sky for all to see.

May you never fall from collective memory.

May your name be spoken evermore with love and reverence.

Hail Loki,

Friend.

Brother.

Force of Change.

I see you. I honor you.

I adore you.

RITUALS FOR SIGYN

This ritual is based on the one I led at East Coast Thing 2019. It was the first year for which Sigyn had a vé, and the first public blót for her in the Northeast Heathen Community. I wanted to do something special, to incorporate a unique element for her that would set this apart from the standard "pass the horn" format we typically use. The weeks leading up to this were spent fretting over whether or not I should write a formal ritual or do my usual freeform style; a decision hadn't yet been made, even as I stood at her vé ten minutes before everyone gathered for the blót.

That's when she told me what to do. Sigyn's gentle voice whispered in my ear it seemed: "Use the bowl."

"Well, of course I'm using the bowl. We pour all of our libations into the bowl!"

"No, use the bowl in place of the horn."

She told me that instead of passing the horn, I needed to pour the offerings into her bowl, and pass the bowl around the circle. By lifting the bowl from her vé, we would be lifting it from her hands and giving her the opportunity to rest and enjoy the blót. As people offered their thanks and hailed her, each drink would lessen the weight of the bowl and lighten the burden of her arms.

I was awestruck by her instruction—I could never in a million years come up with something half as clever, appropriate, or meaningful. It was a tremendous honor to carry out the ritual as she'd requested, and afterward I was overwhelmed by the intense euphoria—both hers and Loki's, who loves her so—and broke down sobbing. That's when I felt her wrap her arms around me and whisper to me that I was her priestess, bringing her back from the cave. This, of course, made me weep even harder. Thankfully, many of my friends had stayed after the ritual and swooped in to join in the group hug. Oh, I was a mess, but it was a mess born of ecstasy. Sigyn was finally getting her due, and there were so many people there to help hold the bowl.

The blót format which follows can be adapted to many purposes when honoring Sigyn with others. The intent of the ritual can be simply to allow her to rest from her task, to thank her for her examples of loyalty and kindness, or to ask her blessings for a situation which calls for compassion. The example provided is for the intention of offering gratitude and asking her help in providing comfort and assistance to those who are struggling.

Items needed

Altar

Altar cloth

Bowl large enough to hold the mead/beverage that will be passed around to everyone gathered

Mead or fruit wine/non alcoholic fruit beverage. Ensure you have enough that everyone present can have a sip or two during the round of toasts with enough left over to pour out as libation to the gods.

Representation of Sigyn (she also appreciates something to represent her sons and her husband as well)

— • —

SAY: Welcome and thank you for joining us for an act of devotion in which we "hold the bowl" for Sigyn, allowing her the chance to rest. This is a simple meditative act focusing on how we can shield, protect, and comfort the ones we love in these uncertain times. The mead will be poured into Sigyn´s bowl, and as we pass the bowl, please hold it aloft as you reflect on Sigyn and her lessons. After a brief meditation, you may speak your praise or prayer to Sigyn before taking a drink from the bowl. As we drink from the bowl, we will not only lessen the weight that Sigyn bears, and in speaking our thanks to her and making the drink sacred, we symbolically replace the venom with gifts.

Hold the bowl aloft for the invocation.

SAY: Incantation-Fetter, She of the Pouring, Our Lady of the Staying Power, we call to you! Sigyn, join us as we celebrate your quiet devotion to what must be done. Let us hold the bowl for you that you may rest, and delight with us as we fill it with gifts and gratitude. Loki's Joy, Mother of Narvi and Vali, You of the Unconquerable Heart, we adore you. Hail Sigyn!

ALL: Hail Sigyn!

Fill the bowl with the mead or beverage of choice, hold it aloft again.

SAY: May the contents of this bowl be blessed and made sacred as we offer our gifts to Sigyn. Sigyn, you are quiet in your duty. You do what you know must be done for the sake of others without complaint, and you do so without looking for accolades. We see you, and we appreciate that you do for us what you did for Loki. You, Grieving Mother, shoulder the weight of all humanity in its suffering. You bestow on us small acts of kindness, you give us gentle comfort, and you remind us that we are not alone as we face the struggles set before us. North Star, may we look to you for inspiration and guidance for helping to offer the same comfort and support to those around us who suffer, whether it be from isolation or from fear. Even the greatest warriors need your gentle touch as they recover from the battles they fight. You are our comfort, you are our compassion, you are our quiet love and loyalty amidst the chaos. Hail Sigyn!

ALL: Hail Sigyn!

Pass the bowl from hand to hand. Each person should have a moment of quiet meditation as they hold the bowl up, reflecting on the growing weight as their arms grow heavy. Then they can speak if they are so moved, to offer their own recognition of Sigyn and her influence in their life, or to thank her for her dedication to duty. Then they may take a drink from the bowl before passing it to the next person. Just as with a horn, take care to keep enough mead/beverage in the bowl so that no one empties it. All the words spoken over the mead are mingled together and become part of the offering, so refill the bowl as many times as necessary to ensure there is always drink in it as it makes its way from hand to hand.

When the bowl has made its way around back to you, hold it in a moment of reflection, say what you will for Sigyn, and drink.

SAY: Sigyn, wonderful words have been shared over this mead, and we pray that our expressions and reflections today honor you and give you encouragement. May you be strengthened by our words and by our gifts, and may we leave here with your lessons in our minds and hearts so that we may share your quiet gifts with others.

Proceed to the spot you have designated for disposition of the gifts to Sigyn, be it a fire or a tree.

ALL: From the gods to the earth to us, from us to the earth to the gods: a gift for a gift!

SOLO RITUAL TO SIGYN

A common devotional practice for Sigyn is "holding the bowl." It's a simple meditative act, but it's a profound and surprisingly weighty (both figuratively and literally) undertaking. As our mythic knowledge of her relates to her task of keeping a bowl aloft over Loki's face, she seems to be trapped in an unending chore of raised arms bearing a gradually filling vessel that grows heavier over time.

There's a reason why holding one's rifle above one's head is a regular "punishment" in military training; from personal experience, the M16A2 isn't particularly heavy in its own right, clocking in at just under nine pounds. However, when your drill sergeant demands you raise it above your head with both arms fully extended and hold it for, say, ten minutes … you may as well be trying to heft a rhinoceros up by about the sixth or seventh minute. Imagine, then, the burning discomfort that seeps into Sigyn's arms the longer she holds her bowl. She's holding it for far longer than what even the most brutal drill sergeant will demand, and in far more dreary conditions.

My experience during Army Basic Combat Training certainly imbued in me a new respect and sympathy for Sigyn's plight with her bowl. Granted, she has freedom of movement and can shift her weight about, stretch and curl her arms as needed to ease the her cramping muscles, and doesn't have a drill instructor screaming in her face throughout the mythic ordeal (I wouldn't be in the least surprised if Loki occasionally let loose with a few expletives here and there, but it would be a poor decision on his part as Sigyn wouldn't hesitate to simply take a step back and let the venom drip in his eyes for a moment to remind him she's there—voluntarily, at that—to help him). Regardless, the experience is pretty miserable, so a lovely way to honor Sigyn is to "take the bowl" from her so she may rest.

The ritual is simple, but not quite as easy as it sounds. The following is my personal practice, but may be altered as you see fit.

Items needed

Bowl

Candle

Flowers

Idol or representation of Sigyn

Idol or representation of Loki

Music, if so desired.

— ◆ —

SAY: Sigyn, Our Lady of the Staying Power, You of the Unconquerable Heart, I call to you. I see your labor, your quiet dedication to your husband in the dark, and I am awed by your compassion and your loyalty to your beloved. I ask that you relinquish the bowl to me for a time so that you may rest. I will take your place in the cave, catching the venom and sparing Loki pain, that you may step out and feel sunlight on your face and delight in fields of flowers. Sigyn, trust me to protect the burden of your arms from the stinging burn dripping from above as I hold the bowl in your place.

Begin your meditation by lighting the candle to illuminate your journey into the cave. When the time is right, whether you envision yourself reaching Sigyn and Loki or you feel Sigyn's presence, pick up the bowl and hold it up over the Loki idol before you. Keep the bowl raised for the duration of the meditation and reflect on what Sigyn means to you. Think on the small, quiet acts of compassion you can perform in your life, think of the unconditional love you feel for those you've chosen to be in your innermost circle of family and friends. Imagine Sigyn reunited with her sons, delighting in their laughter as they play. Picture Loki sweeping her into his arms, unbound, glad and humbled that she chose him.

As the meditation continues, feel the weight of the bowl grow heavier with each passing moment. Feel her grief at the loss of her sons and her distress at seeing her husband bound to rocks. Take note of the sorrow and despair as the dark, stale air of the cave closes in around you and you hear Loki's groans of discomfort as his muscles cramp and scrape against the stone, and his quiet sobs as he too mourns his children.

The bowl's weight is ever increasing. Reflect on the tremors creeping along your arms, your fingers growing stiff as they curve against the pottery. Roll your shoulders, easing the pain that has been creeping into them, and marvel at Sigyn's strength for undertaking such a misery. Take heart and find hope in the love she has for her husband despite the grief she has suffered because of him. She returns to the cave, but now she sits beside Loki, smoothing his hair back from his face, cupping his cheek in her hand, soothing him with the gift of touch.

Be inspired by her dedication to doing what she knows is right, for doing what she must, even if it means she is forgotten and overlooked—she does it not for accolades, but because she doesn't want her beloved to suffer any more than absolutely necessary. She wants to provide comfort, no matter how small. She wants to offer joy, no matter how fleeting. Sigyn sees beyond the present, knowing that this too shall pass. And when this ordeal is over, she will not forget the lessons she has learned, and she will forever represent the blessings that compassion, loyalty, and unyielding love can offer.

Soon, sooner than you expect, you become aware of Sigyn's readiness to reclaim the bowl. Your arms ache, and though it feels as though you've been standing vigil in her place for hours, in that moment, you might wonder if she's possibly had enough time to rest. Her smile reassures you that she has and reminds you that she is made of stronger stuff than us humans.

Place the bowl at the feet of the Sigyn idol and put your flowers into it.

SAY: I offer these flowers to you, their colors bright and their fragrance sweet, to offer you comfort as you comfort your beloved. May they brighten your time in this place and remind you that I see you, and I remember you, and I will help you as you've helped me. Hail Sigyn!

7
LOKAORð
(FINAL THOUGHTS, OR LOKI'S WORDS)

In a final nod to fun with language, take a moment to appreciate the term *Lokaorð*. If you recall, there are academics who think Loki's name is related to the verb *lúka*, "to end." As such, the word *Lokaorð* can be translated as both "Final Thoughts" and "Loki's Words."

This book began as an act of devotion for Loki and Sigyn, but it's turned into something so much more than that. This process has certainly deepened my relationship with them further as I learned and discovered new quirks and fascinating scholarly theories, and I hope the research I shared does the same for you. Having honest, sometimes difficult conversations with other heathens about their attitudes toward Loki broadened my understanding of their own backgrounds and experiences, and that in turn forged greater trust and respect between us. Building frith and community is what heathenry is all about, and this book certainly helped me to further appreciate the American heathen community and the many extraordinary people who comprise it. My greatest wish is that you too have caught a glimpse of the gifts we can offer to each other and to the gods, no matter where you fall on the Loki spectrum.

Loki is the change-maker, and Sigyn is the compassion throughout the upheaval. Our faith and our practices are constantly evolving with the times, keeping pace with society. My heathenry is vastly different from my father's heathenry, which in turn is a different beast from my grandfather's heathenry. This is how the natural order of things should be; it's a lovely thing to hold to tradition and learn from our history as a religion and community, but we mustn't ever stagnate and do things just because that's the way they've always been done. That's Loki's ultimate lesson: never settle for the status quo, never grow complacent. We deserve better. We can do better. We can be better. Keep moving forward, taking inspiration from our past, and make the community stronger and more welcoming for future generations. We don't owe that to the gods—we owe that to *ourselves* and to our children and to their children. Lokeans aren't the underdogs in the community: we're becoming the ones who hold safe space for the outsiders, the liminal ones, those who defy the accepted order of things because we want a better world. And Sigyn helps us in that endeavor, inspiring the compassion and loyalty and unyielding love for everyone we hold dear.

As I write, Loki is poking at me to emphasize his Final Words: Do better. Be better. And laugh as often as you can. You deserve adventure. You deserve to love and be loved. You're worth it.

Hail Loki! Hail Sigyn! Hail the gods and goddesses all!

— • —

Everything started with my grandpa, and I would be remiss to end this book without a final thank you to him, the old-school heathen from Drammen, Norway, the man who embodied everything about Loki that I hold dear, and everything about Sigyn that I admire. Frank Svendsen was (and is) my favorite person in my father's family because he's the one who best represents joy. Whenever I think of him, I think of his deep belly laugh, the way he'd chortle until his eyes watered and a coughing fit would double him over. I have his eyes and his humor, and extended family members tell me I look just like him, which pleases me to no end. His personality, brilliance, and humor reminds me of Loki, which probably accounts for a recurring dream I've had at several points throughout my life.

I'm at my grandparents' house but no one else is there with me. Standing in the kitchen, something compels me to look out the window over the sink. The spacious, tree-lined backyard teems with *hundreds* of red foxes, and I *know* they're linked to my grandpa. They're here because of him. And because I'm his granddaughter, they're here because of me, too. The foxes are a sea of red and copper and white, a fluff-furred ocean ebbing with black-tipped waves, moving on black sand, their golden eyes gleaming and twinkling in the sunlight: they're here because they love us and want us to know we'll never be alone. They will never leave us. They're here for us, Grandpa and me, and they'll always protect us.

Once, just once, there was more to the dream, like an extended director's cut. I had just started college, and I was in the early stages of returning to heathenry after the Catholic Experiment. This time, while I was standing in the kitchen watching the foxes, my grandpa came in from the foyer and beckoned me to his bedroom. In his room, he had several little wooden figures he'd carved (he, like all of the men in his family, was a skilled carpenter), and he sat me down and told me the stories of the gods. I'd known the myths, of course, and I knew who they were, but I listened closely as he talked about how these were our gods and our friends, and that all these years he'd kept the gods close to us and us close to the gods.

Anyone who's celebrated sumbel with me has heard that phrase before: usually during the ancestor round, I hail my grandpa because he's the one who kept the gods close to us and us close to the gods. I *always* say that in ritual, because those are the very words he spoke to me in my dream with the foxes. Even though it was just a dream, derived from one I'd had before and have had since, it's a profoundly precious memory of him, my Grandpa Frank.

You would think that having this dream multiple times throughout my life would have clued me in to Loki's presence. You'd be wrong. Grandpa may have fondly called me his "little genius," but I'm sure Loki would call me something entirely different for my decades of unawareness.

I haven't been dedicated to him for long, just a few years in a lifetime of loving the gods, but he's *always* been around, trying to remain patient while my devotions were offered to others in the pantheon. I've always been on his side in the American debates regarding him, and I've always poured offerings to him when offering to Óðinn. He's always been present in my mind, and his was one of the first idols I bought and displayed in college. According to my friends, he was the god I spoke of the most, so when I announced I was no longer an Óðinswoman but rather a Lokean, I was met with confusion rather than shock (except from Óðinn—that one-eyed bastard heaved a sigh of relief that still annoys me to this day). Everyone always thought I was Lokean all along, and apparently referred to me as such for years. As usual, I was the last one to know. Like his character says in *American Gods*, "You're slow, but you get there in the end."

The same might be said about the American heathen community. It might have taken us a while to really find our footing, especially where Loki is concerned. We're slow, yes, but we'll get there in the end. We're already so much farther along than we could have dreamed some thirty years ago. It's a privilege and an honor to be along for the ride.

Hail the community!

FURTHER READING

A Practical Heathen's Guide to Asatru. Patricia Lafayllve

This is one of the most highly recommended books in the American heathen community for newcomers who wish to learn more. There's a reason for that: it's written by someone who has been living heathen for quite some time, and it's beautifully researched and breaks down a lot of complicated concepts into very accessible language.

Playing With Fire: An Exploration of Loki Laufeyjarson.
Dagulf Loptson

One of the best books for and about Loki I've come across. I reference Dagulf Loptson's work heavily when I'm planning a public ritual for Loki, and this one is a must have for any Lokean's library.

Norwegian Folktales. Peter Christen Asbjørnsen and
Jorgen Moe

A delightful glimpse into Norse folklore, full of stories about crafty foxes and adventures of the Ash Lad.

The Poetic Edda. Carolyne Larrington translation

Of all the translations currently available, this one stands out as a brilliant blend of accessible language and skaldic poetry. Some translations focus on maintaining the meter and rhythm of the Old Norse verses, others focus on the straightforward interpretation of the language used and ideas being conveyed in modern vernacular. This version does both.

Blood Unbound: A Loki Devotional. Edited by Bat Collazo, published by The Troth

This is a solid collection of poems, prayers, and stories members of The Troth have shared in honor of Loki.

GLOSSARY

Aegir: God of the Sea, host of the feast in *Lokasenna*

Æsir: One of the two primary tribes of deities

Angrboda: Jotun, Queen of Iron-Wood. By Loki, she mothered Jörmungandr, Fenrir, and Hel

Asgard: One of the nine realms, home to the Æsir

Baldr: Son of Óðinn and Frigg, also called the Shining One. Slain by mistletoe despite wards of invincibility. Emerges from Helheim after Ragnarok to lead the remaining gods and goddesses in creating a new, ideal society.

Blót: Offering or sacrifice, act of worship. Name given to rites and rituals in heathenry

Brokkr: Dwarf instrumental in the creation of Mjolnir. Brokkr sewed Loki's mouth shut when he couldn't claim Loki's head as a prize due to a technicality, resulting in the kenning "Scar Lip"

Farbauti: Loki's father. A Jotun whose name can be translated as "Cruel Striker"

Fenrir: Loki's son by Angrboda. A giant wolf, he's bound until Ragnarok, during which he's fated to kill Óðinn

Freyja: Vanic goddess, owner of the falcon cloak Loki uses in several myths

Freyr: Vanic god, Freyja's twin. Recipient of magical gifts in the myth about Sif's hair

Frigg: Óðinn's wife, mother of Baldr

Frith: Security and safety, peace, positive communal relationships

Fultrui: Patron god or goddess

Galdr: "Incantation." A form of magic in the lore involving singing or chanting runic spells

Garb: Historical costuming or clothing, worn by some heathens (particularly stricter reconstructionists) for ritual

Gebo: X-shaped rune of reciprocity. Simplified meaning is "gift for a gift"

Godhi/Goði: Priest

Gythia/Gyðia: Priestess

Havamal: "Sayings of the High One." Collection of Óðinn's handy, dandy wisdom in the Poetic Edda that offers good advice in matters of hospitality, personal relationships, communal relationships, war, magic, and acting honorably

Hearth Cult: Your personal spiritual practice and the deities involved in your devotions

Hel: Goddess of the Dead. Daughter of Loki and Angrboda. Ruler of Helheim

Helheim: One of the nine realms. World of the dead overseen by Hel

Hod: Baldr's brother, the blind god involved in The Mistletoe Incident

Hof: Temple building

Idunn: Goddess, keeper of the Apples of Immortality. When she was kidnapped, the Æsir and Vanir grew old and frail, so her rescue was of utmost importance

Jotun: One of the mythical tribes/races. Giants who are typically at odds with the Æsir and Vanir, but have also married or borne/fathered children with them

Jotunheim: One of the nine realms. Land of the giants

Jörmungandr: Son of Loki and Angrboda. World Serpent who encircles Midgard. Fated to kill Thor at Ragnarok

Kenning: Descriptive phrases used in skaldic poetry to reference people, places, and things. Often used as "nicknames" for the gods and goddesses in contemporary heathenry

Kindred: Chosen spiritual family. "Congregations" or formalized collective of heathens

Laufey: Loki's mother. Unclear if she is a Jotun or Æsir. Also called Nál

Logi: Personification of wildfire. Guest at Utgard-Loki's castle feast who defeated Loki in a speed-eating contest

Lokabrenna: "Loki's torch." Old Norse/Icelandic name for the star Sirius. Also the name of the month long series of devotions and art practiced by Lokeans in late summer time when Sirius is rising

Lokasenna: The myth about the events leading up to
   Ragnarok. Loki goes off the deep end and kills a servant,
   then verbally attacks the gods and goddesses present,
   exposing secrets and unpleasant truths. The end of this
   myth details the punishment in the cave. The only myth
   in which Sigyn is featured.

Midgard: One of the nine realms. Encircled by Jörmungandr,
   this is Earth—*our* Earth

Mjolnir: Thor's Hammer and one of the most important and
   recognizable symbols of heathenry and Norse paganism

Narvi: Son of Loki and Sigyn. Also spelled Nari and Narfi.
   Killed at the end of the Lokasenna by his brother Vali, who
   had been turned into a wolf by the gods. Loki is bound to
   rocks by Narvi's entrails

Nisse/Nisser: Norwegian term for elves, or land and home
   spirits

Noki/Nokian: Someone who is adamantly against Loki and
   his veneration

Óðinn: Highest of the gods and goddesses, known also as the
   Allfather. Knows the prophecies of the end times and does
   whatever it takes to avert it. "The ends justify the means"
   applies to Óðinn. He adopted Loki as a brother by oath but
   disregards the terms of their oath in the *Lokasenna.*

Poetic Edda: Collection of myths and wisdom common to
   Scandinavia and Northern Europe before conversion to
   Christianity. The stories are recorded in skaldic verse. Also
   referred to as the Elder Edda

Prose Edda: Collection of myths common to Scandinavia and Northern Europe before conversion to Christianity. These are written in narrative format and include a lot of personal commentary by the Christian historian, Snorri Sturluson, who first wrote the mythology down for cultural preservation. Also known as the Younger Edda

Ragnarok: The end times. Loki and his family lead Surtr's army of Jotuns to Asgard to wage war against the gods

Sif: Thor's wife, renowned for her golden hair. Loki cuts it off for no reason, and in the process of convincing dwarves to make a wig of gold for her, a competition develops between two families of dwarves that result in the gods gaining their greatest treasures (notably Mjolnir) and Loki getting his big mouth sewn shut

Skaði: Goddess of hunting, skiing, and archery. Jotun, daughter of Thjazi, who goes to Asgard to demand restitution for her father's death. She hangs the venomous serpent above Loki's face at the end of the *Lokasenna*, whose poison Sigyn catches in her bowl

Sleipnir: Loki's son, birthed by Loki himself when he took the shape of a mare. Eight-legged horse Óðinn rides across the realms. Only one of Loki's children who gives him a card for Mother's Day

Snorri Sturluson: Christian poet and historian from Iceland who first committed the Norse mythology to written record in the thirteenth century.

Sumbel: Ceremonial drinking and toasting. Generally performed in three rounds: Gods and Goddesses, Ancestors and Heroes, and Toasts and Boasts. Very informal mode of community bonding and frith building. Sometimes happening spontaneously when a group of heathens gather

Thjazi: Jotun king, Skaði's father. He pressured Loki into helping him kidnap Idunn and her Apples of Immortality, and was killed by the Æsir when Loki stole Idunn back

Thor: God of Thunder, son of Óðinn, husband of Sif. Wields the mighty hammer Mjolnir. Frequently lets Loki tag along on his journeys. Often perceived as being a redhead by readers of the lore. Perceived as being blonde and bearing a striking resemblance to Chris Hemsworth by everyone else. Hemsworth's portrayal is certainly far more clever and witty than Thor. But of course, Hemsworth has a good team of writers feeding him lines while our Thor has to come up with his own retorts.

Thrym: Giant who stole Mjolnir. Thought he was being clever by demanding Freyja as a bride in return for the hammer. He got killed, instead.

Tomte/Tomten: Swedish term for elves, or land and home spirits

The Troth: International organization for inclusive heathens. Good resource for educational programs and networking

Tom Hiddleston: British actor. Famous for his role as the Marvel comic book version of Loki. A lanky ginger, he ironically looks more like Loki than he does in the black wig his costume calls for. Unclear whether Hiddleston is playing Loki or if Loki is playing Hiddleston.

Tyr: God of Justice and Order. Lost his hand to Fenrir because of a necessary lie told in order to bind him

UPG/Unsubstantiated Personal Gnosis: Personal knowledge and understanding about a deity or spiritual concept that is gained through experience or direct communication with deity. UPG is not substantiated by any written or historical records

Vali: Son of Loki and Sigyn. Turned into a wolf and set against his brother Narvi at the end of the *Lokasenna*

Vanaheim: One of the nine realms. Home of the Vanir

Vanir: One of the two primary tribes of deities

Völuspá: Book in the Poetic Edda in which Óðinn visits the Seeress and hears the prophecies of all that's to come.

Vættir: Spirits

Vé: Shrine or sacred place

Weregild: Restitution. Acts or payments equal to the cost of one's transgression

Wyrd: Short definition: personal fate. Long definition: the destinies we create for ourselves through our actions and words, as well as the people with whom we interact

BIBLIOGRAPHY

Andrén, Anders. 2005. "Behind 'Heathendom': Archaeological Studies of Old Norse Religion." *Scottish Archaeological Journal* 27 (2): 105–138. https://www.jstor.org/stable /27917543.

Apel, Thomas. n.d. "Loki." Mythopedia. Accessed October 5, 2020. https://mythopedia.com/norse-mythology/gods /loki/.

Asbjørnsen, Peter Christen, and Jorgen Moe. 1982. *Norwegian Folktales*. New York: Pantheon Books.

Bosworth, Joseph, T Northcote Toller, and A Campbell. 1992. *An Anglo-Saxon Dictionary: Based on the Manuscript Collections of Joseph Bosworth. Supplement*. London; New York: Oxford University Press.

Cawley, Frank Stanton. 1939. "The Figure of Loki in Germanic Mythology." *The Harvard Theological Review* 32 (4): 309–326. https://www.jstor.org/stable/1508020.

Cleasby, Richard, Gudbrand Vigfusson, and George Webbe Dasent. 1874. *An Icelandic-English Dictionary, Based on the Ms. Collections of the Late Richard Cleasby.* Oxford.

Crossley-Holland, Kevin. 2007. *The Norse Myths.* New York: Pantheon Books.

Davidson, H.R Ellis. 1990. *Gods and Myths of Northern Europe.* London: Penguin.

Frakes, Jerold C. 1987. "Loki's Mythological Function in the Tripartite System." *The Journal of English and Germanic Philology* 86 (4): 473–486. https://www.jstor.org/stable /27709903.

French, Kevin. 2014. "We Need to Talk About Gefjun: Toward a New Etymology of an Old Icelandic Theonym." MA Thesis, University of Iceland. https://skemman.is/handle /1946/19599.

Ginevra, Riccardo. 2018. "Old Norse Sígyn (*sei̯ k U̯ -N̥ -Į́ Éh 2 -'she of the Pouring'), Vedic °sécanī-'pouring', Celtic Sēquana and PIE *sei̯ k U̯ -'pour'*." Edited by David Goldstein, Stephanie Jamison, and Brent Vine. *Acadamia.Edu* . https://www.academia.edu/38197759/The_Old_Norse _theonym_S%C3%ADgyn_seikw_n_i%C3%A9h_she_of _the_pouring_Vedic_Sanskrit_s%C3%A9can%C4%AB _pouring_the_Celtic_river_name_and_theonym _S%C4%93quana_present_day_river_Seine_France_and _Proto_Indo_European_seikw_pour_Loki_and_Fire _n_2_.

———. 2020. "How Linguistics Helps Us Reconstruct Ancient Fire Mythology." The Philological Society Blog. October 6, 2020. https://blog.philsoc.org.uk/2020/06/10

/how-linguistics-helps-us-reconstruct-ancient-fire-mythology/.

Grundy, Stephan. 2015. *GOD IN FLAMES, GOD IN FET-TERS : Loki's Role in the Northern Religions.* The Troth.

Guerber, H. A. 1909. "Myths of the Norsemen: From the Eddas and Sagas." Www.Gutenberg.org. 1909. https://www.gutenberg.org/files/28497/28497-h/28497-h.htm#pb229. Myths of the Norsemen: From the Eddas and Sagas, 1909.

Heide, Eldar. 2009. "More Inroads to Pre-Christian Notions, After All? The Potential of Late Evidence." In Á *Austrvega: Saga and East Scandinavia: Preprint Papers of the 14th International Saga Conference.* https://www.academia.edu/2401032/More_inroads_to_pre_Christian_notions_after_all_The_potential_of_late_evidenceEl.

———. 2011. "Loki, the Vätte, and the Ash Lad: A Study Combining Old Scandinavian and Late Material." *Viking and Medieval Scandinavia* 7 (January): 63–106. https://doi.org/10.1484/j.vms.1.102616.

Hollander, Lee M. 1988. *The Poetic Edda.* University Of Texas Press.

Jochens, Jenny. 1989. "'Völuspá: Matrix of Norse Woman-hood.'" *The Journal of English and Germanic Philology* 88 (3): 344–362. https://www.jstor.org/stable/27710187.

Kaliff, Anders. 2005. "The Vedic Agni and Scandinavian Fire Rituals. A Possible Connection." *Current Swedish Archaeology* 13: 77–97. https://www.academia.edu/19085449/The_Vedic_Agni_and_Scandinavian_Fire_Rituals_A_Possible_Connection.

Kamenetsky, Christa. 1972. "Folklore as a Political Tool in Nazi Germany." *The Journal of* American Folklore 85 (337): 221. https://doi.org/10.2307/539497.

Kroonen, Guus. 2013. *Etymological Dictionary of Proto-Germanic.* Leiden: Brill.

Lafayllve, Patricia M. 2013. *A Practical Heathen's Guide to Ásatrú.* Woodbury: Llewellyn Publications.

Liberman, Anatoly. 1994. "Snorri and Saxo on Útgarðaloki, with Notes on Loki Laufeyjarson's Character, Career, and Name." in Word Heath = Wortheide = Orðheiði : Essays on Germanic Literature and Usage (1972-1992). Episteme Dell'Antichità E Oltre. Rome: Editrice il Calamo: 176–234.

Lindow, John. 2002. *Norse Mythology: A Guide to Gods, Heroes, Rituals, and Beliefs.* Oxford University Press.

Loptson, Dagulf. 2014a. "A New Place for Loki, Part I." Polytheist.com. September 17, 2014. http://polytheist.com /orgrandr-lokean/2014/09/17/a-new-place-for-loki-part-i/.

———. 2014b. "A New Place for Loki, Part II." Polytheist. com. September 23, 2014. http://polytheist.com/orgrandr -lokean/2014/09/23/a-new-place-for-loki-part-ii/.

———. 2019. *Playing With Fire: An Exploration of Loki Laufeyjarson.* Lulu Enterprises.

Maestas, Silence. 2016. *Worshipping Loki: A Short Introduction.*

Moosbrugger, Mathias. 2010. "Recovering the 'Snorra Edda': On Playing Gods, Loki, and the Importance of History." *Contagion: Journal of Violence, Mimesis, and Culture* 17: 105–120. https://www.jstor.org/stable/41925319.

Neijmann, Daisy, ed. 2006. *A History of Scandinavian Literatures. 5, A History of Icelandic Literature.* S.L.: University of Nebraska Press, Cop.

Olrik, Axel. 1908. "Loki in Recent Folklore." Heimskringla. No. Danske Studier. 1908. https://heimskringla.no/wiki /Loke_i_nyere_folkeoverlevering_%28De_vestlige _nybygder%29.

Paxson, Diana L. 2005. *Taking up the Runes: A Complete Guide to Using Runes in Spells, Rituals, Divination, and Magic.* Boston, Ma: Weiser Books.

Rood, Joshua. 2020. "Investigations into Ásatrú." *AURA— Tidsskrift for Akademiske Studier Av Nyreligiøsitet* 11 (1): 81–95. https://doi.org/10.31265/aura.359.

Schnurbein, Stefanie von. 2000. "The Function of Loki in Snorri Sturluson's 'Edda.'" *History of Religions* 40 (2): 109–124. https://www.jstor.org/stable/3176617.

Snook, Jennifer. 2015. *American Heathens : The Politics of Identity in a Pagan Religious Movement.* Philadelphia: Temple University Press.

Staff. 2019. "11 Things to Know about the Present Day Practice of Ásatrú, the Ancient Religion of the Vikings." Icelandmag. January 22, 2019. https://icelandmag.is /article/11-things-know-about-present-day-practice -Ásatrú-ancient-religion-vikings.

Sturluson, Snorri. 1996. *Edda.* Translated by Anthony Faulkes. London: Everyman.

———. 2005. *Norse Mythology.* Translated by Jesse L Byock. Penguin.

————. 2016. *Poetic Edda.* Translated by Carolyne Larrington. Oxford University Press.

"Völuspá - Norse and Germanic Lore Site with Old Norse /
English Translations of the Poetic Edda and Prose Edda."
n.d. Www.Völuspá.org. Accessed December 1, 2020. http://
www.Völuspá.org/nafnathulur1-20.htm.

World Nuclear News. 2010. "World Nuclear Association -
World Nuclear News." Www.World-Nuclear-News.org.
December 23, 2010. https://www.world-nuclear-news.org
/WR_New_ship_for_Swedish_nuclear_transport_2312101
.html.

INDEX

To Write to the Author

If you wish to contact the author or would like more information about this book, please write to the author in care of Llewellyn Worldwide Ltd. and we will forward your request. Both the author and the publisher appreciate hearing from you and learning of your enjoyment of this book and how it has helped you. Llewellyn Worldwide Ltd. cannot guarantee that every letter written to the author can be answered, but all will be forwarded. Please write to:

Lea Svendsen
℅ Llewellyn Worldwide
2143 Wooddale Drive
Woodbury, MN 55125-2989
Please enclose a self-addressed stamped envelope for reply,
or $1.00 to cover costs. If outside the U.S.A., enclose
an international postal reply coupon.

Many of Llewellyn's authors have websites with additional
information and resources. For more information,
please visit our website at http://www.llewellyn.com.